Functional Skills
English

City & Guilds – Level 2

Getting ready for the City & Guilds Level 2 Functional Skills English test? This fantastic CGP book covers everything you need... and nothing you don't!

Every topic is clearly explained, along with all the reading and writing skills you'll need. There are plenty of questions to help build up your confidence, including two realistic practice papers — with answers for everything at the back of the book.

How to access your free Online Edition

This book includes a free Online Edition to read on your PC, Mac or tablet. You'll just need to go to **cgpbooks.co.uk/extras** and enter this code:

4021 1792 0623 0487

By the way, this code only works for one person. If somebody else has used this book before you, they might have already claimed the Online Edition.

CGP — still the best! ☺

Our sole aim here at CGP is to produce the highest quality books — carefully written, immaculately presented and dangerously close to being funny.

Then we work our socks off to get them out to you — at the cheapest possible prices.

Contents

Part 1 — Reading

Section One — How Ideas Are Presented

Section Two — Finding Information From Texts

The Reading Test

Part 2 — Writing

Section One — Writing Structure and Planning

Published by CGP

Editors:
Tom Carney
Becca Lakin
Rebecca Russell
James Summersgill
Sean Walsh

With thanks to Emma Crighton for the proofreading.

With thanks to Jan Greenway for the copyright research.

Acknowledgements:
Obesity statistics on page 39 copyright © 2019, Health and Social Care Information Centre.
The Health and Social Care Information Centre is non-departmental body created by statute,
also known as NHS Digital. Licensed under Open Government Licence v3.0.

ISBN: 978 1 78908 400 9

Printed by Elanders Ltd, Newcastle upon Tyne.
Clipart from Corel®

What is Functional Skills English?

Functional Skills are a set of qualifications

1) They're designed to give you the **skills** you need in **everyday life**.

2) There are **three** Functional Skills **subjects** — **English**, **Maths** and **ICT**.

3) You may have to sit **tests** in **one**, **two** or all **three** of these subjects.

4) Functional Skills has **five levels** — **Entry Level 1-3**, **Level 1** and **Level 2**.

This book is for Functional Skills English

1) There are **three** parts to Functional Skills English — **reading**, **writing** and **speaking, listening and communicating**.

2) To get a Functional Skills English qualification, you need to **pass all three parts**.

3) This book covers the **reading** and **writing** parts of **Functional Skills English Level 2**.

The papers for each exam board are slightly different — ask your teacher or tutor to make sure you know which one you're sitting.

There are two tests and a controlled assessment

1) **Speaking, listening and communicating** is tested by a **controlled assessment** in class.

2) Reading and writing are tested in **two separate tests**.

3) You might take your test on a **computer** (onscreen) or on **paper**.

Reading

- In the **test**, you have to **read two texts** and **answer questions** on them.

- Some questions might be **multiple choice** (you choose the correct answer).

- Some questions might ask you to **write** your **answer**.

- You **don't** have to write in **full sentences**.

- You **won't** lose marks if you make **spelling**, **punctuation** or **grammar mistakes** in what you write, but make sure your answers are **clear** and **understandable**.

Writing

- In the **test**, you will be asked to write **two texts**.

- These **two texts** will usually be **different**, for example a **letter** and an **article**.

- You **will lose marks** if your spelling, punctuation or grammar are **incorrect**.

2100812

How to Use this Book

This book summarises everything you need to know

1) This book is designed to help you **go over** what you're already learning in class.

2) Use it along with any **notes** and **resources** your teacher has given you.

3) You can work through this book from **start** to **finish**...

4) ...or you can just **target the topics** that you're **not sure** about.

Use this book to revise and test yourself

1) This book is split into **two parts** — **reading** and **writing**.

2) The topics in each part are usually **spread over two pages**:

Here's the title of the topic.

On the left-hand page there's all the important information for each topic.

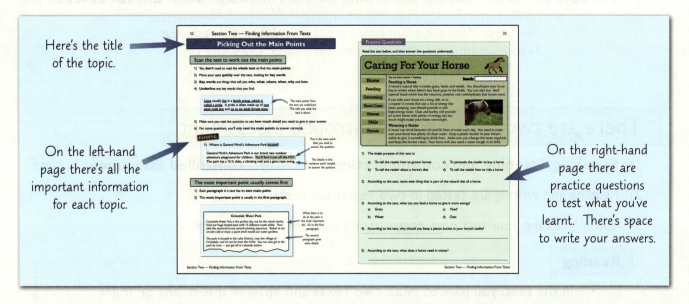

On the right-hand page there are practice questions to test what you've learnt. There's space to write your answers.

There are answers to all the practice questions and the practice papers at the back of the book.

There's lots of test-style practice

1) There are **practice papers** at the **end** of both parts of the book.

2) These papers are based on **actual Functional Skills English assessments**.

3) This means that the questions are **similar** to the ones you'll get in the **real tests**.

4) They're a good way of **testing** the **skills you've learnt** under **timed conditions**.

5) This will give you a **good idea** of what to expect when you take the real test.

Using a Dictionary

You can use a dictionary in the reading paper

1) You can use a dictionary to look up the **meaning** of a **tricky word** at any time in the reading paper.

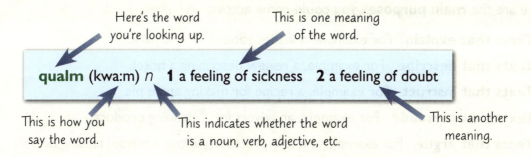

Here's the word you're looking up.

This is one meaning of the word.

qualm (kwa:m) *n*   **1** a feeling of sickness   **2** a feeling of doubt

This is how you say the word.

This indicates whether the word is a noun, verb, adjective, etc.

This is another meaning.

2) You **won't** be allowed to use a dictionary in the **writing paper**.

Practise using a dictionary before the test

1) The words in a **dictionary** are listed in **alphabetical order**.

2) That means all the words beginning with '**a**' are **grouped together**, then all the words beginning with '**b**' and so on.

3) Each **letter** in the word is also listed in **alphabetical order**.

4) When you're looking up a word, check the words in **bold** at the **top** of **each page**.

5) These words help you work out which **page** you need to **turn to**.

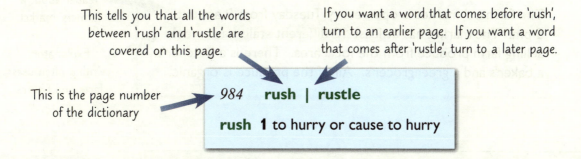

This tells you that all the words between 'rush' and 'rustle' are covered on this page.

If you want a word that comes before 'rush', turn to an earlier page. If you want a word that comes after 'rustle', turn to a later page.

This is the page number of the dictionary

984   **rush | rustle**

rush 1 to hurry or cause to hurry

Don't use a dictionary all the time

1) Dictionaries can be **helpful**, but **don't** use them **too often**.

2) Looking up **lots** of words will **slow you down** in the test.

3) Try looking at the **rest of the sentence** to **narrow down** what a tricky word could mean.

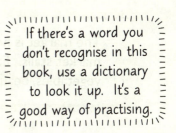

If there's a word you don't recognise in this book, use a dictionary to look it up. It's a good way of practising.

The Purpose of Texts

Texts have different purposes

1) Every text has a **purpose**. A **purpose** is the **reason** why the text has been written.

2) Here are the **main purposes** you could come across:

- **Texts that explain**. For example, a leaflet about a theme park.
- **Texts that describe**. For example, a review describing a hotel.
- **Texts that instruct**. For example, a recipe for making apple pie.
- **Texts that persuade**. For example, an advert for a cleaning product.
- **Texts that argue**. For example, a letter protesting about a school closing down.
- **Texts that discuss**. For example, a report about how much traffic is on the roads.
- **Texts that advise**. For example, a webpage telling you how to save money.
- **Texts that entertain or amuse**. For example, an article about a funny real-life event.
- **Texts that enquire**. For example, an email to a restaurant asking about their menu.
- **Texts that inspire**. For example, a webpage with ideas for children's party games.

3) These **aren't** the **only** ones, so don't panic if something unexpected comes up in the test.

Explanatory texts tell you about something

Explanatory texts are full of **facts**. **Facts** are statements that can be **proved**.

> The farmers' market is open every Tuesday from 9 am until 5 pm. The market has at least 12 different stalls each week selling farm produce from the local area. There is a butcher's, a baker's and a greengrocer's. All of the produce is organic.

This text is informing the reader about a farmers' market.

Explanatory writing often uses facts and figures.

Texts that describe help you imagine something

Descriptive writing uses lots of **adjectives** (describing words).

> The market is held on a wide street filled with market stalls. Each stall is overflowing with fresh vegetables, beautiful cakes or colourful jars of jam.

This text is describing a market.

Adjectives like 'wide', 'fresh', 'beautiful' and 'colourful' help you imagine what the market is like.

Practice Questions

Read the text below, and then answer the questions underneath.

Stanhead Community Choir

We are a local choir who rehearse at Stanhead Community Centre. We rehearse between 7 and 9 pm on Tuesday evenings. The choir is made up of 80 people between the ages of 16 and 85. There is also a junior choir for children aged 6 to 16. The junior choir rehearses on Saturday mornings at 9 am.

Our history:

The choir is a charitable organisation that was set up in 2008 by Mark Patel. Mark was the conductor of Stanhead Choral Society. He wanted to create a choir that would attract people from all walks of life and would bring people from all over Stanhead together.

How it works:

People can come to the choir to learn to sing as part of a large group. We sing a mixture of popular and choral music. You don't need to be able to read music to join.

Performances:

We perform at the Stanhead Festival every year. We also perform carols in the town square at Christmas and sing at the county show in May.

For more information, visit our website.

1) Find the **main** purpose of this text, then select some text to support your answer.

Main purpose .... *to get ... in the top head Community Centre.*

Example from the text .... *He wanted to create a choir that would attract people.*

2) Name two places where the choir performs.

Place 1: *Stanhea Festival*

Place 2: *Town Square*

3) In what year was the choir started?

2008.

The Purpose of Texts

Persuasive texts try to convince the reader to do something

1) Persuasive texts sometimes use **words** that make the reader **feel** something.

2) They might also use **facts** to sound more **convincing**.

This text is trying to persuade the reader to buy a new phone.

> **Trevina X4600**
>
> The outstanding new X4600 is sleek, easy to use and reliable. It has a number of excellent features including accurate GPS tracking. You can pinpoint your location to within 20 m. It even lets your friends know where you are so you can find each other in a crowd! The Trevina X4600 is the future. It's the smartest phone around. Get yours now!

Words like 'outstanding', 'sleek' and 'excellent' impress the reader.

Texts that argue want the reader to agree with an opinion

1) Texts that argue make **one opinion** very clear.

2) They often use **facts** to back up the argument and forceful language to show how they feel.

The writer's opinion is clear from the start.

> The tracking technology installed with the new Trevina X4600 is a disgrace. It allows **anyone** with your phone number to know exactly where you are at any time. There are already over 10 000 cases of stalking each year. Tracking technology is bound to make this worse.

Facts help to back up the argument.

Strong words, like 'disgrace', show how angry the writer is.

Texts that discuss a topic use evidence to reach a conclusion

1) Texts that discuss give **more than one opinion**.

2) They often look at **both sides** of an argument and reach a **conclusion**.

> There has been a lot of criticism of the new Trevina X4600. I agree that the GPS technology would make it easier to follow or even stalk someone. However, I am impressed by the accuracy of the GPS function and it would be useful sometimes to see where your friends are. Overall, the X4600 is an excellent example of modern technology.

The text is balanced because it gives two different opinions.

The text finishes with a conclusion.

Practice Questions

Read the text below, and then answer the questions underneath.

Opinions

Minna Williams is a disgrace   *Jo Timms*

I couldn't believe my ears yesterday when I heard Minna Williams speaking on the radio. The wife of the American politician Truman Williams said quite clearly that she thought women should stay at home and shouldn't work. She also said that women who do work 'don't deserve to be paid the same as men'. Is she really prepared to go back on hundreds of years of fighting for equal rights?

Minna Williams is a housewife with five children. She has never worked. That is her choice and it is fine by me. But what she said yesterday was completely unacceptable. She implied that women are weaker than men in every way and do not deserve to be recognised as equals. Millions of women all over the world work to support themselves and their families. Women are just as capable as men, and should be paid exactly the same as men in the same jobs.

In some countries today, women are treated like second-class citizens. They are not even given the opportunity to learn or to work. Mrs Williams has grown up in a country where she is treated as an equal and where she could choose to work or not. She is one of the lucky ones, but she is encouraging young women to throw away those opportunities. She is a disgrace and needs to educate herself before giving her opinions to the public.

1) According to the text, what does Minna Williams say?

   a) Women are second-class citizens   c) Women should be paid more than men

   b) Women shouldn't work   d) Women should be treated as equals

2) The writer thinks that:

   a) Minna Williams is right   c) Minna Williams is a second-class citizen

   b) Minna Williams should get a job   d) Minna Williams is wrong

3) What is the full name of Minna Williams's husband?

....

4) Find the **main** purpose of this text, then select some text to support your answer.

   Main purpose ....

....

   Example from the text ....

....

The Purpose of Texts

Texts that instruct tell you exactly what to do

1) Texts that instruct give the reader **instructions** to follow.

2) They are often split up into **numbered lists** or **bullet points**.

3) They use **clear language** so they are easy to understand.

> • Deal out seven cards to each player.
>
> • Each player may discard one card that they do not want.

Simple language makes these instructions easy to follow.

Each instruction has a separate bullet point.

Texts that advise suggest how to do something

Texts that advise give you **tips** about something.

> **HOW TO CHOOSE A NEW CAR**
> Here are some top tips for choosing a new car.
> • Think about how much you want to spend. Having a budget makes it easier to choose what car to buy.
> • Think about what you need it for. For example, if you have a big family, you'll need a large car.

These sentences are giving advice. They are suggesting how to do something.

Texts can have more than one purpose

1) Sometimes texts have **two or more** purposes.

2) For example, a text might **persuade** and **explain**, or **explain** and **describe**.

> Lighthouse UK helps homeless people in the UK. Many of them have problems with alcohol and drugs, but they all deserve a chance. We run drop-in centres where homeless people can feel safe, get help and learn new skills. A donation of £3 a month helps us change lives. Change a life. Support Lighthouse UK.

This text explains about Lighthouse UK.

It also persuades you to donate to Lighthouse UK.

Read the texts below, and then answer the questions underneath each one.

Sporting success leads to increase in road cycling

The British cycling team were very successful at the Cycling World Championships this summer. The British team picked up 12 gold medals, 4 silver medals and a bronze medal at the championships in Hamburg, Germany. Since then, there has been a noticeable rise in the number of people out and about on their bikes.

Cycling is popular for a number of reasons. It's cheap, it's a great way to get around and it keeps you fit. David Branford of the British cycling team said, "It's fabulous to see so many people enjoying cycling. Cycling is a fantastic sport. I'd like to see more kids getting involved, then Britain can continue to succeed internationally at cycling in the future."

So why not have a go yourself? Most people have a bike lying around in a shed or garage. Get it out, fix it up and get out and about. Cycling couldn't be easier. It's just like riding a bike!

1) Find **two** purposes of this text. Choose an example from the text to support your answer.

Purpose 1 ....

Example ....

....

Purpose 2 ....

Example ....

....

Weekend Guide to Paris — Sight Number 5

5. The Eiffel Tower

The Eiffel Tower is an architectural beauty. People come from all over Europe to see the best view in Paris from the top of the tower. You can see the elegant Louvre art gallery, the River Seine snaking its way through the heart of the bustling city and the bridges filled with people and traffic. The view is unforgettable. Sadly, so are the queues. If you don't want to wait for 2 hours to get to the top you need to get there early. Young, fit people might consider climbing the stairs to avoid queuing for the lift. Tickets cost between €2.50 and €25.

2) Find **two** purposes of this text. Choose an example from the text to support your answer.

Purpose 1 ....

Example ....

....

Purpose 2 ....

Example ....

....

Reading Between the Lines

Facts are statements that can be proved

1) Some texts contain **facts** and **statistics**.

2) Statistics are **facts** that are based on **research** or **surveys**.

3) Statistics are usually written as **numbers** or **percentages**.

4) Phrases like '**experts say**', '**research shows**', and '**surveys show**' often introduce facts.

> The population of Angleston is increasing. Research shows that 20% of the population is under the age of 16. The population is bound to continue to increase.

This is a fact.
It can be proved.

This is a statistic. It is a percentage based on data from research.

This is not a fact.
It cannot be proved.

An opinion is something the writer thinks

1) Opinions **aren't** true or untrue. They are just **beliefs** and **can't** be proved.

2) Phrases like '**I think**', '**I believe**' or '**many people say**' show a statement is an opinion.

> I think music should be available to download for free. It's important that everyone has access to music.

'I think' shows this is an opinion.

This is another opinion. It's the writer's belief.

It can be hard to tell the difference between fact and opinion

1) If you're **not sure** whether something is a fact or an opinion, think about whether it can be **proved** or not. If it **can**, it is a **fact**. If it **can't**, it is an **opinion**.

2) Opinions can be **presented** to look like facts. This makes them seem more **believable**.

> The majority of companies would be more efficient if they spent more money on IT.

This sounds factual, but it can't be proved.

Practice Questions

1) Read each statement and write 'fact' or 'opinion' next to each one to say whether the statement is **presented** as a fact or an opinion.

   a) 'Research shows that 60% of the UK population are overweight' .... *Fa...*

   b) 'Women are generally better at DIY than men' .... *Op*

   c) 'I think 9 out of 10 people would say they like chocolate' .... *Op*

   d) 'Surveys show that children with siblings are better at sharing' .... *Fact*

Read the text below, and then answer the questions underneath.

The success of the smoking ban

In July 2007, smoking was banned in public places in England. This was the most sensible decision made by the government in years. The ban was popular with the majority of the population. In a survey, 78% of people said they still support the smoking ban.

It is now much more pleasant to go into a pub or a restaurant. Before the ban, pubs were filled with smoke which made you cough and made your hair and clothes smell. However, according to a study, 16% of bar and pub owners noticed a significant drop in business when the ban was introduced because smokers were staying at home rather than going out for a drink.

Making smoking in public places illegal has had a positive impact on people's health. Since the ban, nearly 2 million people in the UK have given up smoking and the number of heart attacks has fallen by more than 40%. The benefits have also affected non-smokers. For example, the number of children suffering from chest infections has decreased by 20%.

---

2) There are six statements from the text in the table below. Put a **tick** next to each statement to show which are presented as **facts** and which are presented as **opinions**.

	Fact	Opinion
In July 2007, smoking was banned in public places in England	✓	
This was the most sensible decision made by the government in years		✓
In a survey, 78% of people said they still support the smoking ban	✓	
It is now much more pleasant to go into a pub or a restaurant		✓
Since the ban, nearly 2 million people in the UK have given up smoking	✓	
The number of children suffering from chest infections has decreased by 20%	✓	

3) Give **another** example of a statistic from the article that is **not** in the table.

....

....

....

Reading Between the Lines

Writing isn't always balanced

1) Sometimes a writer has a **point of view** (an opinion) they want to get across.

2) They try to **influence** the reader by only giving their **opinion**. This is called **bias**.

3) You can spot bias in a text if the writer **exaggerates** something or **ignores** the other side of the argument.

> North Coast Trains is the worst train company in Britain. Their trains are never on time, and they are always overcrowded. Last week I had to stand for a six-hour journey, which was just great.

The first sentence is an opinion. Many people might disagree with it.

The text ignores the fact that other train companies have trains that aren't on time and are overcrowded.

The writer doesn't actually mean it was great. They mean the opposite. This is irony. Here it makes the reader understand how angry the writer is feeling.

4) Bias isn't always **obvious**. A writer might seem to talk in a **neutral** way, but only actually give one **point of view**.

Biased texts use different methods to influence the reader

1) A text might use **humour** to **entertain** the reader. This makes the reader **like** the writer.

> The new Hadawi sports car is the worst car I've ever driven. The engine is pathetic — I think my three-legged tortoise could probably move faster.

This is a funny image. If the reader likes the writer, they are more likely to agree with their opinion.

2) Biased texts might use **forceful language** to make the reader **agree** with the writer.

> My meal was dreadful — the meat was stringy and disgusting.

These words exaggerate how bad the food really was.

3) Biased texts might make claims that **aren't supported** with **evidence**.

> Everyone was delighted by the plans for a new car park.

It seems unlikely that everyone was delighted.

Practice Questions

Read the texts below, and then answer the questions underneath each one.

WARHURST WINS AGAIN

Michael Warhurst, the Independent candidate for Gawesbury, has been elected for the third year in a row. Mr Warhurst is the best MP Gawesbury has ever seen. He campaigned against the closure of Gawesbury General Hospital and fought the opening of a new Metromarket supermarket which threatened businesses and shops in the town centre. Mr Warhurst will continue to campaign for the interests of the people of Gawesbury with the support of all the locals.

---

1) Find **one** way the writer has tried to influence the reader's opinion from the text above. Support your answers with examples from the text.

Way the writer has tried to influence the reader ....

....

Example from the text ....

....

← → [   ] ↻ ⌂

🎨 beauty reviews online

Mane-tame Shampoo   Reviewed by Jane Ryan ★☆☆☆☆

I'd heard good things about this shampoo so I bought a bottle last week, but sadly I was thoroughly disappointed. Not only was I absolutely outraged by the price, but the product itself smelt horrendous. Despite the hideous smell, I tried washing my hair with it this morning, but it made my hair greasier than a plate of chips. I will not be buying this shampoo again.

---

2) Find **two** ways the writer has tried to influence the reader's opinion from the text above. Support your answers with examples from the text.

First way the writer has tried to influence the reader ....

....

Example from the text ....

....

Second way the writer has tried to influence the reader ....

....

Example from the text ....

....

Understanding the Writer's Point

Work out the writer's argument

1) The writer's argument is their **point of view**.

2) You can usually work out the writer's point of view by looking at the **language** they use.

3) Sometimes, writers state things **clearly**.

> Working in an office during the summer is horrible.

The writer clearly states that they find office work during the summer 'horrible'.

4) Other times, the writer's meaning isn't clearly stated — you have to **figure it out**.

> Changes to office working conditions during the summer are long-overdue.

The writer doesn't say that they dislike working in an office, but saying that change is 'long-overdue' implies that they are unhappy with the current conditions.

5) Writers often use both **facts** and **opinions** in their argument to get their point across.

6) Writers can **develop** their argument by giving **several reasons** for their opinion.

> Furthermore, the temperature during the summer can become extremely high. It's difficult to concentrate in such uncomfortable conditions. Air-conditioning could really improve productivity.

The writer gives another reason for their opinion.

This shows what the writer thinks should change about their workplace.

You may need to compare how different writers feel

1) In the **test**, you'll read texts by different writers.

2) You'll probably have to compare the **information** and **opinions** from different texts.

EXAMPLE:

1) Give one difference between the writers' opinions in these texts.

Text A
I get the bus every day. In all my years of taking the bus to town, I've met more people than I can count, and many of them have become lifelong friends.

Text B
I have to get the bus to work every morning. I waste half an hour sitting there listening to other passengers talking a load of nonsense.

The language used shows that the writers have different opinions. The writer of Text A has made 'lifelong friends', which shows they have a positive opinion. The writer of Text B feels negatively. They think their fellow passengers talk 'nonsense'.

Practice Questions

Read the texts below, and then answer the questions underneath.

Text A

Video Games Replacing Face-to-Face Contact

Gone are the days of kids hanging out with their mates after school, cycling to the local park and spending pocket money on sweets. Now, the moment they finish school, youngsters prefer to rush home to play the latest shooting game while talking to their friends online. Surely the lack of direct contact can't be good for them, and playing these mind-numbing violent games encourages anti-social behaviour. At least they are still talking to their friends online and getting some social interaction. However, the lack of face-to-face contact will almost certainly make it harder for these teens when they enter the workplace and need to speak to their colleagues.

Text B

'I earn money for doing what I love' — an interview with a video games tester

A number of people have asked me recently why I play video games for a living. Well firstly, I think video games are a work of art. Some of them are beautiful and others are educational — I've learnt so many new things from the games I've played. It's also a great opportunity to connect with different people around the globe.

1) Find **two** problems the writer of Text A has with video games.
   Choose quotations from the text to support your answers.

   Problem 1 ....

   Quotation ....

   Problem 2 ....

   Quotation ....

2) Give one opinion that is the **same** in Text A and Text B, and one that is **different**.

   Same opinion ....

   ....

   Different opinion ....

   ....

Spotting Different Types of Text

Letters and emails are sent to other people

1) Letters have **addresses**, a **date** and a **greeting** at the top, and a **sign-off** at the end.

2) Emails have a '**to**' and a '**from**' box at the top, as well as a box for the email's **subject**.

Adverts and leaflets try to grab your attention

1) Adverts are usually **persuasive**. They try to **convince** you to do something.

2) Leaflets are usually **explanatory**. They give you **information** about something.

3) Adverts and leaflets both use **colours**, **pictures** and different **fonts** to get **noticed**.

An interesting font and logo grab the reader's attention.

Colour makes the leaflet look attractive.

Bullet points keep information simple and easy to read.

Websites have specific features

They usually have a **search box** and links to other **webpages**.

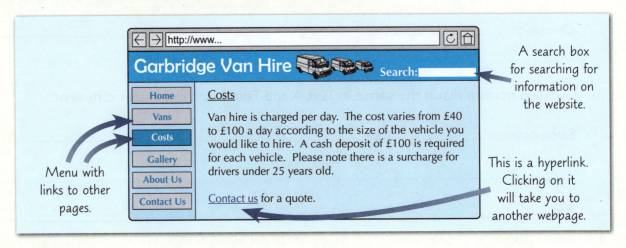

Menu with links to other pages.

A search box for searching for information on the website.

This is a hyperlink. Clicking on it will take you to another webpage.

Spotting Different Types of Text

Articles are in newspapers or magazines

1) They have **headlines** to tell you what the article is **about**.

2) **Subheadings** and **columns** are used to break up the text.

Practice Questions

Look at the four text types below, and then answer the questions underneath each one.

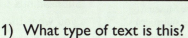
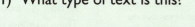

1) What type of text is this?

....

2) Name **one** feature that tells you this.

....

3) What type of text is this?

....

4) Name **one** feature that tells you this.

....

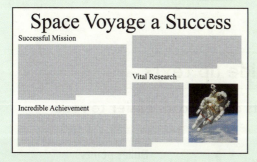

5) What type of text is this?

....

6) Name **one** feature that tells you this.

....

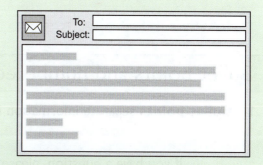

7) What type of text is this?

....

8) Name **one** feature that tells you this.

....

Spotting Presentational Features

Different texts have different presentational features

1) Texts can be **laid out** using different **features**, like **headlines** and **bullet points**.

2) These are called **presentational** (or **organisational**) **features** and they make a text **easier to understand**.

3) Presentational features can also affect the way you **read** and **interpret** a text.

Headlines and subheadings tell you what a text is about

1) **Headlines** and **titles** are always at the **top** of the page in a bigger font.

2) They try to **grab** the reader's **attention** and get them to read the text.

3) **Subheadings** tell you what a section of a text is about.

This is a headline. It's eye-catching.

Man arrested following gemstone robbery

A man has been arrested on suspicion of stealing a set of precious gemstones from a stone museum in Cumbria. Simon Renwick, 45, was arrested at his home in West Lawick on Saturday morning.

Thief deactivated burglar alarm

The robbery was carried out in the early hours of the morning at the Gemstone Museum on Walltree Drive last Wednesday. The stolen gems were part of a unique display in the museum and are said to be worth over £100,000. Police say that the thief managed to break in through the main entrance and successfully deactivate the burglar alarm.

Police appeal for witnesses

Police are appealing for any witnesses who noticed anything unusual at the museum on the night of the robbery.

Subheadings tell you what that section is about. They also break up the text.

Columns make the text easier to read.

Bullet points and numbered lists divide up texts

1) **Bullet points** separate information into **short** bits of text so it's **easier** to **read**.

If you have a question, please contact us by:
- Emailing us at flixstationery@azmail.co.uk
- Phoning us on 08081 570 543

Bullet points separate each piece of information. This makes the writing clear.

2) **Numbered lists** can be used instead of bullet points.

3) This is usually for things that are **in a set order**, such as a set of **instructions**.

Practice Questions

Read the texts below, and then answer the questions underneath each one.

(A)

Noah's bark to the rescue

By Fatima Dove

A pensioner's dog is being praised for bravery during last week's flooding at Low Bridge. The dog's barking attracted the attention of the fire service who came to rescue his owner, 72-year-old Mrs Wallace.

Dog barked in rain for three hours

Mrs Wallace was suffering from flu and was sleeping as the floodwaters rose around her house on Riverside Lane. When she woke up, she was trapped upstairs. She tried to shout for help out of the window, but her voice was too quiet against the roar of the river. Her 8-year-old Labrador, Noah, climbed onto the windowsill and began to bark. After 2 hours firemen working nearby heard the dog and came to investigate. Noah stayed on the windowsill barking until Mrs Wallace was rescued by helicopter an hour later.

"I could have died if it wasn't for Noah."

Mrs Wallace was taken to Bridgedale Community Hospital where she was treated for shock. She said afterwards, "Noah was my saviour. I could have died if it wasn't for him".

Noah was cared for by a local animal shelter until he could be returned to Mrs Wallace.

(B)

(C)

1) a)   Name presentational feature A ....

   b)   Give **one** reason why it is effective ....

   ....

2) a)   Name presentational feature B ....

   b)   Give **one** reason why it is effective ....

   ....

3) a)   Name presentational feature C ....

   b)   Give **one** reason why it is effective ....

   ....

(D)

There are a number of reasons why it's important to check your bank balance regularly:

- You will have a better idea of how much money you are spending.
- You are less likely to go overdrawn on your account.
- You can make sure all your payments have been made.
- You are more likely to notice fraud on your account.

4) a)   Name presentational feature D ....

   b)   Give **one** reason why it is effective ....

   ....

Spotting Presentational Features

Graphics and captions help you understand a text

A **graphic** is a **picture**, **diagram** or **chart**. It shows you what the text is about.

Third Oil Spill Hits French Coastline

The third oil spill in four weeks has hit the north-west coast of France. The oil was released from a tanker which ran aground in the Atlantic, 30 miles offshore. Beaches along the coast have been closed to the public while the clean-up process takes place.

Volunteers clean a beach near Carnac after the spill.

The graphic shows people cleaning up the oil spill. It helps the reader imagine the situation.

Graphics also make the text more interesting to read.

A caption is a bit of text that tells you more about the graphic. It makes it clear what the graphic is about.

Colour affects how you read a text

1) Colourful **text** and **backgrounds** have an effect on the reader.

2) **Bright colours** make text look more **fun**.

3) **Dark colours** create a **serious mood** suitable for more **formal** texts.

Fonts help set the tone of a text

1) **Serious, formal** fonts are for **serious, formal** texts.

2) **Cartoony, childish** fonts are for **light-hearted** texts, or texts for **children**.

3) Some words might be highlighted in **bold** or in *italics* to make them **stand out**.

Five Top Tips for **FIRE SAFETY**

1 Install a **smoke alarm**

2 Make an **action plan** in case of fire

3 Blow candles **out** if you leave a room

4 **Stub out** cigarettes carefully

5 Keep matches and lighters **away** from children

In the event of a fire dial 999 immediately.

The colour red is connected with danger. It also makes the text stand out.

The graphic helps the reader know what the text is about before they have even read it.

This is in italics to make it look different from the rest of the text. It makes the reader look at it first.

The bold text makes the most important information stand out.

Practice Questions

Look at the texts below, and then answer the questions underneath each one.

Mr Clean

Great value carpet cleaning!

Mr Clean can remove **any mark** or **stain**.
Customer satisfaction guaranteed.

*"My carpets looked like new after Mr Clean had seen to them.
His service was reliable and great value for money."* Mrs Jones, Birtley.

Call **01632 960778** now for a quote.

£10 per hour!

Ⓐ Ⓑ Ⓒ

1) The text marked A is in bold. Give **one** reason why this is effective.

....

....

2) Give **one** reason why the graphic marked B is effective.

....

....

3) Why do you think the text marked C is in italics?

a) To show you what the text is about

c) To show it's different from the rest of the text

b) To show that it is informative

d) To make it blend with the rest of the text

HOMEWARE SALE — 50% OFF

At Fratton Homes, we've cut prices on everything in store.
It's your chance to grab a great bargain:

- 50% off all bedding
- 50% off kitchenware
- 40% off all curtains
- 35% off beds and mattresses

FRATTON HOMES

4) Identify **two** presentational features in this text.

Feature 1 ....

Feature 2 ....

5) Choose **one** and give **one** reason why it is effective.

....

....

Spotting Presentational Features

Text boxes make text stand out

Text boxes can be used to make important information **stand out** — this makes it **easier** to **find**.

> ### Your Company Car
>
> To help you do your job, you will be offered a company car. You will be able to choose your car from a list of options. The company will pay your fuel expenses up to 8000 business miles per year.
> You will be expected to keep your car clean and well-maintained.
> We also expect employees to drive safely and carefully at all times.
>
> > When deciding if you wish to take up the offer of a company car, please be aware that it will be a taxable benefit. Please read this document for more information.

The text box catches the reader's eye because it stands out.

Tables organise information

1) Tables show information in **rows** and **columns**, which makes it **easier to understand**.

2) Tables are useful for presenting large amounts of **complicated data** in a **clear** way.

Footnotes add extra information

1) Footnotes appear at the bottom of the page.

2) Footnotes give **definitions** or extra **information** without **interrupting** the main text.

Look for the 1 in the footnotes to find the information.

> Our business is the market leader[1] but we need to continue growing to keep this position.
> _____
> [1] We currently hold a 37% share of the market, with our competitor holding a 29% share.

This means there is extra information about this sentence.

Footnotes are usually numbered.

Footnotes can also be shown by symbols (like an asterisk *).

Glossaries and keys explain words or diagrams

1) **Glossaries** contain a list of **key words** with **explanations** of what they mean.

2) A **legend** (or **key**) is a set of **labels** that tell you what a diagram means.

This book has a glossary. It's on pages 141 and 142.

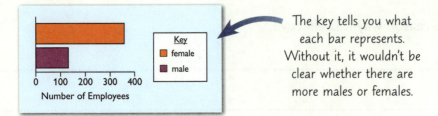

The key tells you what each bar represents. Without it, it wouldn't be clear whether there are more males or females.

Practice Questions

Read the text below, and then answer the questions underneath.

New Vacuum Cleaner 'Air Action 3000' Set To Launch

You are here: Home > Staff Area > News

Search: [   ]

36 Months In The Making

When our design team first presented their ideas for the 'Air Action 3000' three years ago, some of us were nervous about such an ambitious project. As a relatively small company, we didn't know if we had the manpower or machinery to make this new vacuum cleaner a success.

An Uphill Battle

Despite a number of complications in developing the new vacuum, we've got a fantastic finished product that we're immensely proud of. It's been a team effort, so thank you to everyone involved.

Key Features
- Most powerful vacuum cleaner on the market
- Four-hour battery life
- RRP £239.99

	Predicted Sales (thousands)
Year 1	120
Year 2	60
Year 3	40

The Product Launch

We've got big plans to launch this product. We're advertising in national newspapers and have a big TV campaign planned. We're hoping this will help us to sell more than 100 000 units in our first year.

---

1) What is the text about?

   ....

   ....

2) Give **two** presentational features that the text uses.

   Feature 1 ....

   Feature 2 ....

3) Choose **one** and give **one** reason why it is effective.

   ....

   ....

4) Give **one other** presentational feature this text could use to make it easier to understand.

   ....

Spotting Language Techniques

Texts use different techniques to persuade the reader

1) A **direct address to the reader** is when it sounds as if the writer is **speaking directly** to the reader.

2) This makes the text seem more **personal**, which may help to **persuade** the reader.

> You will never forget your day out at Kentmere Water Park.

Words such as 'you' and 'your' make it seem as though the text is addressing the reader personally.

3) **Rhetorical questions** are questions which don't need an **answer**.

4) They are used to try and persuade the reader to **agree** with the writer.

> Is it right that footballers are paid such vast sums of money? They certainly work hard, but so do nurses and teachers.

The question suggests that the reader should say 'no'. The writer is trying to make the reader agree with their point of view.

5) **Emotive language** can be persuasive because it appeals to the reader's feelings.

> Donate just £5 to save these helpless animals.

The word 'helpless' makes the reader feel sorry for the animals — this means that they are more likely to donate.

Adverts often use slogans to persuade the reader

1) Slogans are **short**, **memorable** phrases used in **advertising**.

2) **Alliteration** is used in slogans to make them **catchy** and easy to **remember**.

3) Alliteration is when words that are **close together** begin with the **same sound**.

> Mickey's Motorhomes — making holidays memorable.

The 'rule of three' is used to create emphasis

1) The **'rule of three'** is when a writer uses a **list** of **three words** or **phrases** in their writing.

2) They do this to **emphasise** the point they are making.

3) This technique is often used in **persuasive writing**.

> The film was entertaining, engaging and touching.

This list of three positive adjectives emphasises the writer's positive feelings about the film.

Section One — How Ideas Are Presented

Practice Questions

Read the two texts below, and then answer the questions underneath each one.

Yewbarrow Castle

Is there a better way to spend a day than exploring Yewbarrow Castle? With its impressive building, fascinating history and breathtaking surroundings, there is something for everyone to enjoy. The castle is full of surprises, including secret passages and hidden doors — who doesn't like getting lost now and again? Yewbarrow Castle is well worth a visit, and we want as many people as possible to experience our beautiful castle, its beautiful grounds and the beautiful landscape.

1) Which **two** persuasive techniques are used in this text?

   a)   Rule of three   c)   Rhetorical question

   b)   Direct address to the reader   d)   Alliteration

2) Give **one** example from the text of each technique.

....

....

BILLY'S BIKES
Builders of Beautiful Bikes

Here at Billy's Bikes, we specialise in creating your dream bike. If you have something special in mind, come and talk to us and we'll do our best to make it a reality. We just love the look on our customers' faces when they see their new bike for the first time!

We're also experts when it comes to sticky gears, squeaky brakes and rusty chains. So if you have any problems with your bike, bring it straight to us. We will do all we can to fix it for you. And don't forget, we're known across the country as Builders of Beautiful Bikes.

3) 'Builders of Beautiful Bikes' is an example of:

   a)   Rhetorical question   c)   Alliteration

   b)   Direct address to the reader   d)   Rule of three

4) Write down the names of **two** other language techniques used in the text.

....

....

Spotting Language Techniques

Metaphors and similes are used to describe things

1) Metaphors and similes help the reader to **imagine** what the writer is describing.

2) A **metaphor** is a way of describing something by saying **it is** something else.

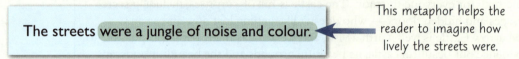

The streets were a jungle of noise and colour.

This metaphor helps the reader to imagine how lively the streets were.

3) A **simile** is a way of describing something by **comparing** it to something else.

4) Similes often use words such as '**like**' or '**as**' to make comparisons.

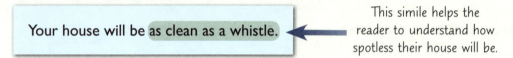

Your house will be as clean as a whistle.

This simile helps the reader to understand how spotless their house will be.

5) Metaphors and similes can strengthen the writer's **argument** and make the text's **purpose** clearer.

The new Vixen Mop glides across the floor like a skater across ice.

This simile strengthens the writer's argument that it is a good mop — this makes the text more persuasive.

Idioms are commonly used sayings

1) Idioms are phrases with a **set meaning** that is **different** from the **literal meaning** of the words.

2) For example, 'it's raining **cats and dogs**' is an idiom which means 'it's raining **heavily**'.

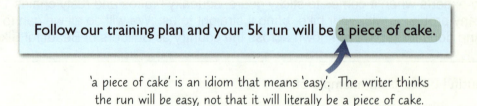

Follow our training plan and your 5k run will be a piece of cake.

'a piece of cake' is an idiom that means 'easy'. The writer thinks the run will be easy, not that it will literally be a piece of cake.

3) Writers use idioms to make their writing more **entertaining** and **interesting**.

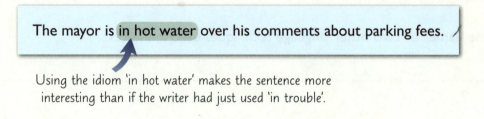

The mayor is in hot water over his comments about parking fees.

Using the idiom 'in hot water' makes the sentence more interesting than if the writer had just used 'in trouble'.

Practice Questions

1) Read each sentence and write next to each one whether it is a simile, a metaphor or an idiom.

   a) The hotel staff did whatever we asked at the drop of a hat. ....

   b) The stadium was a cauldron of nerves and anticipation. ....

   c) The film was as dull as a grey afternoon. ....

Read the text below, and then answer the questions underneath.

← → [   ] ⟳ ⌂

📖 **Novel News Online**

Take Fire to the Mountain

Tomorrow, Lee Nightingale's new novel *Take Fire to the Mountain* will finally be released, and I am on the edge of my seat. His last novel, published 16 years ago, had a huge impact on me — it was a tornado which hurtled into my life, changing it forever. As I wait for his new novel to drop through the letterbox, I feel like a child about to open their birthday presents. Nightingale is such a talented author — his novels transport me to another world. Waiting for a book to be released is like getting ready to set off on an adventure, and I have a feeling this is going to be a good one. Also, someone has let the cat out of the bag that Nightingale is working on another novel. How exciting!

---

2) 'it was a tornado which hurtled into my life' is an example of:

   a) A metaphor

   b) An idiom

   c) A simile

   d) A rhetorical question

3) How does the language technique in Question 2 help to express meaning?

   ....

   ....

4) Write down the meaning of the idiom 'let the cat out of the bag'.

   ....

5) Give **one** example of a simile from the text.

   ....

Identifying Tone and Style

Writers have their own voice

1) All writers have their own **individual** way of writing. This is called the **writer's voice**.

2) The writer's voice is a combination of the **language**, **style** and **tone** of their writing.

Writing can have a personal or impersonal tone

1) **Personal** writing sounds like it is **talking to the reader**.

2) It's written from the writer's **point of view**, so it's full of **opinions** and it shows **emotion**.

> I was delighted to hear that the council are going to improve the cycle lanes. It means I will be able to cycle to work safely.

Personal writing gives the writer's opinions — it says what they think.

It uses words like 'I', 'we' and 'you'.

3) **Impersonal** writing **doesn't** tell you anything about the writer's **personality**.

4) It just reports the **facts**, so it's usually **neutral** and doesn't take anybody's **side**.

> Some local people have welcomed the council's plans to improve the cycle lanes. It means they can cycle to work safely.

Impersonal writing doesn't usually give any opinions.

It uses words like 'she', 'him' and 'they'.

Writing can be formal or informal

1) **Formal** writing sounds **serious**. It usually has an **impersonal tone**.

2) It is used for things like **articles** and **job applications** because it **sounds** more **professional**.

> The substitute goalkeeper had to play in lieu of Xiang, who had suffered an injury in the first half.

'in lieu' is a formal way of saying 'instead'.

'who had' is a more formal way of saying 'who'd' — shortened words aren't used in formal writing.

3) **Informal** writing sounds **chatty**. It usually has a **personal** or **conversational tone**.

4) It is used for things like **letters** to your **friends** or **family** because it's more **friendly**.

> Don't throw your back out! Make sure your boss gives you all the right training if you have to lift stuff at work.

Informal writing uses shortened words and slang. For example, it uses the word 'boss' instead of 'manager'.

Practice Questions

Read the text below, and then answer the questions underneath.

Ivan and Tania are getting hitched!

Love
is
in
the
air

Dear ___Sanjay___

We're getting married on Saturday 14th July and we'd love you to come and celebrate with us.

Where: St John's in the Valley, Bridgeley

When: One o'clock

We want our wedding to be a really fun and relaxed day. The wedding reception is going to be in the church hall and we're going to have a bouncy castle and games to play outside. There'll be a barbecue and plenty of food and drink to go around. We'd like everyone to stay for the evening and dance their socks off.

Dress Code: Please come in whatever you feel most comfortable wearing. If you want to wear jeans, feel free.

Presents: We're going to Mauritius on our honeymoon. We'd be really grateful if you could contribute to our honeymoon fund.

Please let us know if you can come by emailing **ivanandtania@azmail.co.uk**

1) a) Is the tone of this invitation personal or impersonal? ....

   b) How can you tell?

   ....

   ....

2) The text suggests that:

   a) The wedding is going to be serious   c) The dress code is very formal

   b) The wedding is going to be casual   d) The reception will only be held outside

3) a) Is this invitation formal or informal? ....

   b) How can you tell?

   ....

   ....

4) Why do you think it has been written in this way?

   a) To make Sanjay feel excited   c) It matches the style of the wedding

   b) It is a wedding invitation   d) To give information clearly

Identifying Tone and Style

An explanatory style tells the reader about something

1) An explanatory text often includes **technical** or **specialist** language (see page 70).

2) It has an **impersonal tone** and **doesn't** usually **include** the writer's **opinion**.

Elderly At Risk Of Identity Theft

Identity theft is on the rise, with almost 500 people falling victim to fraudsters every day. Senior citizens are often seen as 'easy targets' by scammers, as they are generally less aware of the strategies used by online criminals.
One common tactic that criminals use is called 'phishing'. Phishing is where the fraudster pretends to be from an official institution and sends the victim a fake website, telling them to enter their details. The fake website records the victim's details, giving the criminal access to their finances.

The writer will often include explanations of technical language.

The writer gives statistics about the topic.

The writer gives facts without stating their opinion on them.

An advisory style tells the reader how to do something

1) An advisory text tells the reader **what to do**.

2) **Clear**, **simple** language makes the instructions **easy to understand**.

Whisk the eggs and sugar until the mixture thickens. Then, gradually add flour. Use a sieve to avoid any lumps.

Command words are common in advisory texts.

A humorous writing style makes the reader laugh

1) Writers might use humour to **persuade** the reader to agree with their point of view.

2) Writers can create humour using **exaggeration**, **repetition** and **informal language**.

3) **Sarcasm** is where the writer means the **opposite** of what they say.
   It has a **negative** tone, so it's often used to **criticise** something.

The plans for the new factory are nothing short of brilliant — I can't wait for the new building to spoil the lovely view from my window. I'll now have a sea of bricks to look at for the rest of time.

The writer uses sarcasm to show that they don't think the factory is a good idea.

The use of exaggeration persuades the reader to agree with the writer's point of view.

Practice Questions

Look at the three texts below, and then answer the questions underneath each one.

Changing a Light Bulb

Start by turning off the electricity at the fuse box, not just at the wall switch.

Ensure you let the bulb cool before you touch it. Push the bulb gently upwards and twist anti-clockwise to remove.

Replace the bulb, then turn the power back on. Wrap the old bulb in paper before putting it in the bin.

My friend and I went camping last week. I told him we should pack insect repellent, but he insisted we didn't need it. One night, a mosquito the size of a helicopter came into the tent. We couldn't catch it and he got about a million bites. Should've brought that bug spray...

1) What type of writing style is this?

....

2) Name **one** feature that tells you this.

....

3) What type of writing style is this?

....

4) Name **one** feature that tells you this.

My
....

Robots Replace Workers

Robots are appearing more and more in our day-to-day lives, from robotic lawn mowers to self-driving cars. They're also entering our workplaces too.

A robot is a machine that is programmed to do a specific job. They can be used for repetitive tasks which don't require human decision-making. Some companies are already using robots for certain jobs, and many plan to use them more. For example, one manufacturing company in China intends to replace 90% of the workforce with robots by 2022.

5) What type of writing style is this?

impersonal   informal
....

6) Name **two** features that tell you this.

....

....

Picking Out the Main Points

Scan the text to work out the main points

1) You **don't** need to read the **whole text** to find the **main points**.

2) Move your eyes **quickly** over the text, looking for **key words**.

3) **Key words** are things that tell you **who**, **what**, **where**, **when**, **why** and **how**.

4) **Underline** any key words that you find.

> <u>Lions</u> usually <u>live</u> in a <u>family group, which is called a pride</u>. A pride is often made up of <u>one adult male lion</u> and <u>up to six adult female lions</u>.

The main points from the text are underlined. This tells you what the text is about.

5) Make sure you read the question to see **how much detail** you need to give in your answer.

6) For some questions, you'll only need the **main points** to answer correctly.

EXAMPLE:

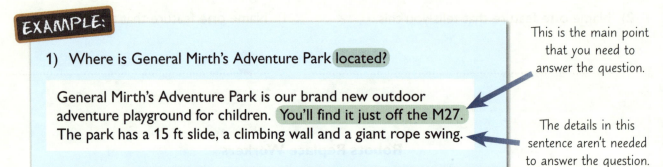

1) Where is General Mirth's Adventure Park located?

General Mirth's Adventure Park is our brand new outdoor adventure playground for children. You'll find it just off the M27. The park has a 15 ft slide, a climbing wall and a giant rope swing.

This is the main point that you need to answer the question.

The details in this sentence aren't needed to answer the question.

The most important point usually comes first

1) Each **paragraph** in a text has its **own main point**.

2) The **most important point** is usually in the **first paragraph**.

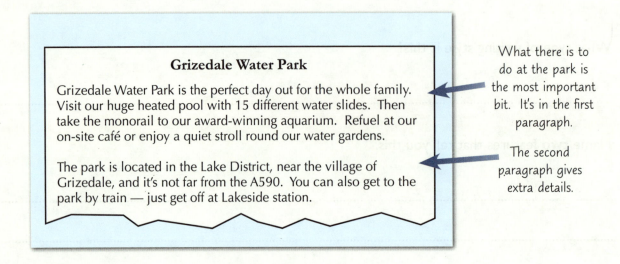

Grizedale Water Park

Grizedale Water Park is the perfect day out for the whole family. Visit our huge heated pool with 15 different water slides. Then take the monorail to our award-winning aquarium. Refuel at our on-site café or enjoy a quiet stroll round our water gardens.

The park is located in the Lake District, near the village of Grizedale, and it's not far from the A590. You can also get to the park by train — just get off at Lakeside station.

What there is to do at the park is the most important bit. It's in the first paragraph.

The second paragraph gives extra details.

Practice Questions

Read the text below, and then answer the questions underneath.

Caring For Your Horse

Home

Feeding

Grooming

Hoof Care

Illness

FAQs

Forum

You are here: Home > Feeding

Search: [ ]

Feeding a Horse

A horse's natural diet includes grass, herbs and weeds. You should give your horse hay in winter when there's less fresh grass in the fields. You can also buy 'feed' (special food) which has the vitamins, proteins and carbohydrates that horses need.

If you take your horse on a long ride, or to compete in events that use a lot of energy like show jumping, you should provide it with high-energy food. Oats and barley will provide an active horse with plenty of energy, but too much might make your horse overweight.

Watering a Horse

A horse can drink between 30 and 50 litres of water each day. You need to make sure your horse has plenty of clean water. Keep a plastic bucket in your horse's stable to give it something to drink from. Make sure you change the water regularly and keep the bucket clean. Your horse will also need a water trough in its field.

1) The **main** purpose of this text is:

   a) To tell the reader how to groom horses   c) To persuade the reader to buy a horse

   b) To tell the reader about a horse's diet   d) To tell the reader how to ride a horse

2) According to the text, name **one** thing that is part of the natural diet of a horse.

....

3) According to the text, what can you feed a horse to give it more energy?

   a) Grass   c) 'Feed'

   b) Water   d) Oats

4) According to the text, why should you keep a plastic bucket in your horse's stable?

....

5) According to the text, what does a horse need in winter?

....

Reading for Detail

It's important for some texts to include specific details

1) While some texts only need to include the main points, others need **specific details**.

2) For example, a writer might add details to a **report** to make it more thorough or useful.

The layout of a text can help you find details

1) **Organisational features** like titles and subheadings tell you **where** to find information.

2) Use them to decide which **part** of a text to **check first**.

3) Then **scan** that part of the text to find the **details** you're looking for.

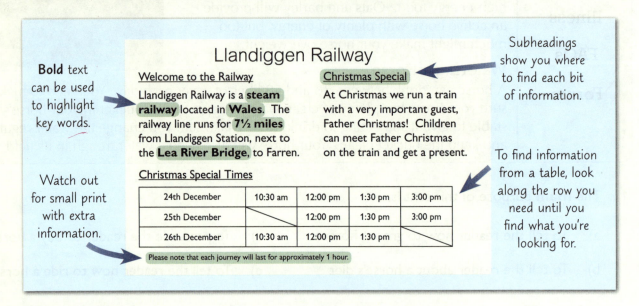

Bold text can be used to highlight key words.

Watch out for small print with extra information.

Llandiggen Railway

Welcome to the Railway

Llandiggen Railway is a **steam railway** located in **Wales**. The railway line runs for **7½ miles** from Llandiggen Station, next to the **Lea River Bridge**, to Farren.

Christmas Special

At Christmas we run a train with a very important guest, Father Christmas! Children can meet Father Christmas on the train and get a present.

Subheadings show you where to find each bit of information.

Christmas Special Times

24th December	10:30 am	12:00 pm	1:30 pm	3:00 pm
25th December		12:00 pm	1:30 pm	3:00 pm
26th December	10:30 am	12:00 pm	1:30 pm	

Please note that each journey will last for approximately 1 hour.

To find information from a table, look along the row you need until you find what you're looking for.

The information you need can be tricky to find

The **information** you **need** from a text might be in things like **graphs**, **charts** and **tables**.

EXAMPLE:

1) What is the most popular after-school activity?

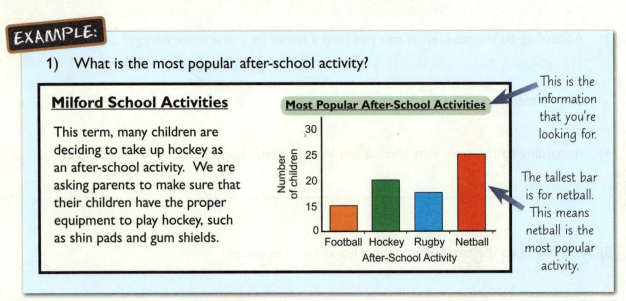

Milford School Activities

This term, many children are deciding to take up hockey as an after-school activity. We are asking parents to make sure that their children have the proper equipment to play hockey, such as shin pads and gum shields.

Most Popular After-School Activities

This is the information that you're looking for.

The tallest bar is for netball. This means netball is the most popular activity.

Practice Questions

Read the text below, and then answer the questions underneath.

Massive Furniture Sale!

At Furnish Plus, we've gone sale crazy and slashed the prices on all our leading ranges. But you'll have to hurry. These amazing sale prices will only be available on April 28th.

Great Deals

Just look at some of the extraordinary deals on furniture you can get at Furnish Plus:

Item	WAS	NOW	SAVING
Standford Office Desk	£149.99	£99.99	33%
McIntyre Classic Dresser	£899.99	£599.99	33%
Brockwell 3-seater Sofa	£750.00	£375.00	50%

More Offers in Store

There are loads more offers in the store. Come down and have a look for yourself. You'll find us at 48 Morley Road, Smithsgate Retail Park.

Get here early to avoid the queues!

Comfee Armchairs only £99!

1) When is the sale being held?

........28th........April..

2) Name the organisational feature used to present the prices of the furniture.

........Table..

3) Which item of furniture is the most expensive after the discount?

    a)   Standford Office Desk   c)   Comfee Armchair

    b)   Brockwell 3-seater Sofa   d)   McIntyre Classic Dresser

4) How much did the Brockwell 3-seater Sofa cost before the discount?

    a)   £149.99   c)   £750.00

    b)   £99   d)   £899.99

5) Name **one** item of furniture that has a saving of 33%.

........Desk........Dresser..

Using Information

A summary is a brief description of the important points

1) A summary sometimes comes at the **start** a text, for example in an article.

2) It introduces the **important points**.

> This article is about physical education in schools and its importance to children's health. It will also look at how physical education teaches children about teamwork and co-operation, which are skills that everyone needs.

These are the most important points in the text.

3) A summary sometimes comes at the **end** of a text, for example in a report.

4) It can **sum up** an argument and give the writer's **opinion**.

> Opening a new library will mean that we will all have to pay more council tax to fund it. However, the educational benefit of the library will be good for everyone. That is why I think it would be an excellent idea to open a new library.

The first two sentences summarise the main points.

The last sentence gives an opinion.

A text might require you to respond to something

1) Different texts will require you to **respond** in **different ways**.

2) A text might ask for you to **write a comment** or **confirm something**.

3) Others might ask you to **call** a **phone number**, **write** to an **address** or **visit** a **website**.

EXAMPLE:

> 1) How can you find more information about adopting an orangutan?
>
> For just £5 a month, you can adopt an orangutan and help pay for the food needed at the orangutan's sanctuary. To find out more about adopting an orangutan, please call us on 08081 570081.

You need to call the phone number to find out more information about adopting an orangutan.

Practice Questions

Read the text below, and then answer the questions underneath.

Fury Over New Housing

Hendley Council have given their support to controversial plans for a new luxury housing estate. This has caused outrage among the residents of Hendley.

The London firm Hythes Housing will build the multi-million pound estate on the site of the derelict playground near to St Paul's churchyard. Local residents had hoped that this site would be used for a new children's play area.

When the decision was announced, about thirty people gathered outside the council offices and jeered at the councillors when they emerged. The protests were led by Greg Fisher. He said, "This is a disgraceful decision. Money has won out over the genuine needs of local people. The new play area is desperately needed for the borough's children." Mr Fisher went on to claim that the councillors had "dollar signs in their eyes".

Councillor Carol Swann responded, "We know that feelings are running high over this issue, but we are confident we can reach a solution that is acceptable to everyone." She described the development as an "exciting new scheme" from which "everyone will benefit, including local people."

If you would like to have your say on this issue, please visit our online forum.

1) Who is going to build the new luxury housing estate?

 a) Hendley Council   c) Greg Fisher

 b) Hythes Housing   d) Carol Swann

2) Where in Hendley will the new housing estate be built?

....

3) How can you give your own opinion on the new housing estate?

....

4) What does Greg Fisher think should be built instead of the new housing estate?

....

5) Write down **two** things that Carol Swann said about the new housing estate.

 1 ....

 2 ....

Using More Than One Text

You might need to use more than one text

1) One text may **not** give you all the information that you need.

2) Sometimes you'll have to use **more than one** text to get **all** of the information.

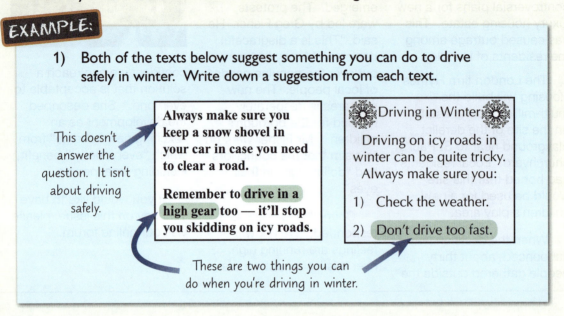

EXAMPLE:

1) Both of the texts below suggest something you can do to drive safely in winter. Write down a suggestion from each text.

This doesn't answer the question. It isn't about driving safely.

> Always make sure you keep a snow shovel in your car in case you need to clear a road.
>
> Remember to drive in a high gear too — it'll stop you skidding on icy roads.

❄️ Driving in Winter ❄️

Driving on icy roads in winter can be quite tricky. Always make sure you:

1) Check the weather.

2) Don't drive too fast.

These are two things you can do when you're driving in winter.

Look for similarities and differences between texts

1) You could be asked to **compare** two different texts.

2) You might need to compare:

- the **information** they give to the reader

- the **ideas** and **opinions** they express

EXAMPLE:

1) Find two examples from each text to show that the writers give similar advice for finding a job.

Text A

> **Volunteers Needed**
>
> Stressing about your job? Well AgriOpps is here to help.
>
> Don't worry — our commitment-free voluntary positions take the stress out of trying something new. Try them and find a career you love today.
>
> Email agriopps@azmail.co.uk for more information.

Both texts encourage the reader not to get stressed.

Both texts recommend volunteering to try and find something you enjoy.

Text B

> Careers Advice Monthly
>
> Starting out in the world of work doesn't have to be scary. Here are some helpful tips to get you started:
>
> - Turn your hobby into a job.
>
> - Try something new by volunteering.
>
> - Apply for an internship.

Read the texts below, and then answer the questions underneath.

Text A

'Fitter Together' Support Group

'Fitter Together' lets you make friends and get fit.

You'll find friends to exercise with, e.g:

- People to walk to work with.

- Gym buddies for moral support.

Join now and start getting 'Fitter Together'!

I ❤ BEING HEALTHY

Looking after your heart is really important.

Here are some top tips for a healthy heart:

- Give up smoking.

- Exercise regularly.

- Reduce your salt intake.

Text B

ALMOST A THIRD OF THE UK IS OBESE

A recent report has identified that almost 30% of adults in the UK are classified as obese. The report also states that only 18% of UK children eat enough fruit and vegetables each day.

Doctors recommend roughly 150 minutes of aerobic exercise and two strength workouts a week. They also recommend eating at least five portions of fruit and vegetables a day.

Experts warn that if people don't change their eating and exercise habits soon, they could be at risk from serious health problems such as heart disease, diabetes and some cancers.

1) For each statement below, circle to say whether it is **true** or **false**.

   a) Both Text A and Text B recommend walking to work. **True / False**

   b) Both Text A and Text B mention the risks of not exercising. **True ✓ / False**

   c) Both Text A and Text B suggest exercise keeps your heart healthy. **True ✓ / False**

   d) Neither of the texts recommend trying a new sport. **True ✓ / False**

   e) Both texts encourage people to exercise to get fit and healthy. **True ✓ / False**

2) What does **Text B** recommend that **Text A doesn't**? Circle your answer.

   a) Walk to work instead of drive

   b) Try a new sport

   c) Join a gym

   d) ✓ Eat fruit and vegetables

Using More Than One Text

Sometimes you'll be asked how information is put across

1) It won't always be enough just to **spot** similarities or differences in what the texts **say**.

2) You could be asked **how** information is **conveyed** (or put across) to the reader.

3) Writers use different techniques to **affect the reader** in different ways.

4) For example, humorous language might be used to **entertain** the reader.

5) You might need to **compare** the techniques used in different texts.

EXAMPLE:

1) Which of these statements about the language used in the texts below is correct?

> Do you want to supercharge your CV? Stop by the Function Room on Mayhill Rd on Tuesday for a special session on how to improve your CV and stand out from the crowd.

> Call the number overleaf to book your one-to-one interview practice with a careers adviser.
>
> "You will be more charismatic, confident and calm after just one session!" — Jen, 21

a) Both use quotations to support their points.

b) Both use direct address to appeal to the reader.

c) Both use formal language to seem serious.

d) Both use the rule of three to be memorable.

You might be asked to use quotations

1) Some questions will ask you to **give quotations** to back up the points you're making.

2) Other questions may ask you to **find quotations** from the text.

EXAMPLE:

1) Give one quotation from each text below to show that both writers are disappointed with the cancellation of Sports Day.

Text A

> **SCHOOL BULLETIN**
> It is with regret that we have decided to cancel Sports Day. We cannot adequately supervise all of the children on the field, as a union strike has left the school with only 60% of its teaching staff this week.

Text B

> Dear Mrs Harvey,
> We think you have let everyone down by cancelling Sports Day. Our children are very disappointed. If necessary, we will volunteer time to ensure the event goes ahead.
> Parents of Class 4F

Quotation from Text A: "It is with regret"

Quotation from Text B: "you have let everyone down"

Make sure you copy quotations accurately from the text.

Practice Questions

Text A

<u>Before Your Interview</u>

- Think about areas of your CV you might be asked about and how you can link them to the job you are applying for.

- Prepare answers about your strengths, weaknesses and any relevant work experience you have acquired.

- Come up with some questions to ask at the end about the role or the company, e.g. 'How will I receive feedback?'

Five Common Interview Mistakes to Avoid:	
1	Being rude
2	Dressing inappropriately
3	Not researching the company
4	Not silencing your phone
5	Arriving late

Text B

Interview Success: Tips

1) Speak Up

Try not to give one-word answers to questions. You should always try to add some detail to your points where you can. Just remember to stay polite, and don't waffle.

2) Read All About It

Companies like it when you show that you've learnt about them, so be sure to check out their website. Their history, mission and recent projects are a good place to start.

3) Confidence Is Key

It's okay to feel nervous before an interview — it shows that you care. But you need to act confident even if you don't feel it, e.g. make eye contact, don't speak too fast and don't fidget.

1) a) Which text says that you shouldn't give short answers in interviews? ....

b) Give a quotation to support your answer.

....

2) a) Which text recommends asking questions at the end of the interview? ....

b) Give a quotation to support your answer.

....

3) Use a piece of evidence from each text to suggest one similiarity in the advice given.

....

....

4) For each statement below, circle to say whether it is **true** or **false**.

a) Both texts give quotations to support their arguments. **True / False**

b) Both texts use bullet points or numbered lists to split up information. **True / False**

c) Both texts use direct address to speak directly to the reader. **True / False**

Different Types of Question

Multiple-choice questions give you several possible answers

1) For multiple-choice questions, you'll be given a **range of options**.

2) You have to choose the **correct option**.

3) **Rule out** the **options** that are **definitely wrong** until you're left with the **right answer**.

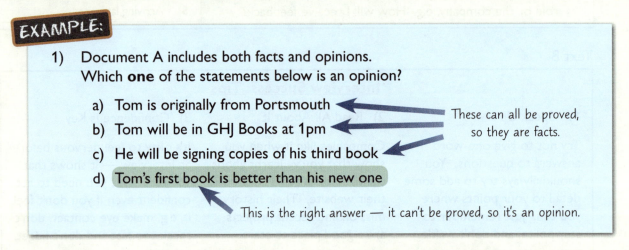

EXAMPLE:

1) Document A includes both facts and opinions.
   Which **one** of the statements below is an opinion?

   a) Tom is originally from Portsmouth
   b) Tom will be in GHJ Books at 1pm
   c) He will be signing copies of his third book
   d) Tom's first book is better than his new one

   These can all be proved, so they are facts.

   This is the right answer — it can't be proved, so it's an opinion.

4) Some multiple-choice questions might ask you to find **more than one** correct answer.

5) Always **check** the question to see **how many** options you have to choose.

Sometimes you'll have to write out your answer

1) Questions which **aren't multiple choice** will have a **space** for you to write your answer.

2) Make sure you **write enough detail** to answer the question **properly**.

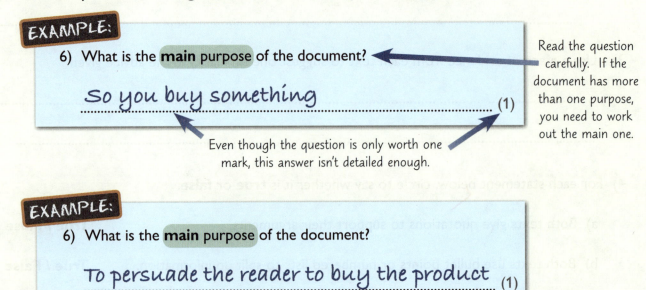

EXAMPLE:

6) What is the **main** purpose of the document?

   So you buy something   (1)

   Read the question carefully. If the document has more than one purpose, you need to work out the main one.

   Even though the question is only worth one mark, this answer isn't detailed enough.

EXAMPLE:

6) What is the **main** purpose of the document?

   To persuade the reader to buy the product (1)

   This answer gives a much clearer and more detailed response.

Different Types of Question

Some questions will involve quotations

1) Some questions might include a **quotation** as part of the question.

EXAMPLE:

9) The writer of Document B says 'Do not let the mixture overheat!'
Give **one** effect that the exclamation mark has on the reader.

It emphasises the importance of the command. (1)

2) Others may ask you to **give a quotation** in your answer.

EXAMPLE:

10) Which informal phrase is used instead of 'refuses to tolerate'?

won't stand for it ← This is a quotation. (1)

EXAMPLE:

11) The writer of Document A thinks that progress has been **slow**.
Give **one** word or phrase from the document that suggests this.

a snail's pace (1)

If you're using a quotation, make sure you write
down **exactly** what appears in the document.

You will have to compare documents

When you are **comparing** documents, make sure you use
examples from **both** documents if you're asked to.

Turn to p.38 for advice
on making comparisons.

15) Compare how ideas about buying a house
differ in Document A **and** Document B.

Make sure your answer includes:

- **one** example from **each** document
to compare how the ideas differ

- **one** example from **each** document to show a similarity
or a difference in how the ideas are **conveyed**.

(4 marks)

The question is asking
you to compare the two
documents and give
evidence to support
your comparison.

The question is
worth four marks, so
you should give four
examples (two from
each document).

Practice Questions

Read the document below, and then answer the questions underneath.

Sports Physio

Mark Pitt

Whatever sport you do, whether it's running, football or swimming, it's likely that you will pick up an injury at some point. By visiting a professional sports physio like me, you can make sure that you'll get fighting fit as soon as possible.

I specialise in dealing with:

- **Strains and sprains** — two of the most common sports injuries. I can help you with any discomfort and speed up the healing process.

- **Back and neck pain** — using a combination of hot and cold compresses, I can loosen up your muscles with a high-intensity shoulder, neck and head rub.

- **Joint pain and arthritis** — I am an old hand at treating more elderly clients, and I have designed a special fitness programme so you can stay in top form even with reduced movement.

I am fully trained with 10 years experience as a physio. I offer professionalism at a rock-bottom price. Contact me at Mark.Pitt@azmail.co.uk or on 0118 4960111 for a free quote or for more information.

1) What is the **main** purpose of this document?

   a) To persuade you to book a physio session

   b) To entertain people who go to the gym

   c) To explain healthy lifestyles

   d) To inform you about exercise

2) Give **one** example of direct address from the document.

....

3) a) Give **one** way you can contact Mark Pitt.

....

   b) Which organisational feature helped you to find this information?

....

4) Which informal phrases does the writer use instead of the following words?

   a) experienced ....

   b) cheap ....

Reading Test Advice

You're not marked on spelling, punctuation or grammar

1) In the **reading test**, you **don't** need to worry about **spelling**, **punctuation** or **grammar** unless you're specifically asked about it.

2) Don't use your **dictionary** too much. Only use it if it will help you **answer** a question.

3) Answers **don't** have to be in **sentences**, but they must answer the **question** fully.

4) Make sure you pick out the **correct information** and that your answer is **clear**.

Read every question carefully

The most important thing to remember is:

Make sure you **answer the question**. Only pick out **relevant information**.

1) Check each question to make sure you're using the **correct document**.

2) Make sure to check whether you need to **compare more than one document**.

Make sure you give two clear differences in how each document puts its ideas across to the reader.

15) Look at Documents A **and** B. Give two differences in how these documents convey their ideas.

3) Use your **time sensibly**. Spend **more time** on questions worth **more marks**.

4) If you're really stuck on a **multiple-choice question**, make a **sensible guess**.

5) Make sure **each point** you write is **separate** and you haven't put the **same thing twice**.

Prepare well for onscreen testing

1) If you're doing your test on a computer, try to do an **onscreen sample test** beforehand.

2) Make sure you know what all the **buttons** do and how the test **works**.

3) Ask your **teacher** or **tutor** for **more information** about what your test will be like.

BLANK PAGE

Functional Skills

English   Level 2

Reading
Road Safety
Source Documents

Time allowed: 1 hour

Information for candidates
- There are **two documents** in this booklet.
- Read **each** document **carefully**.
- You will be tested on **both** documents in the Question Booklet:
  Document A is needed to answer questions 1 to 6.
  Document B is needed to answer questions 7 to 14.
  Both documents are needed to answer question 15.

Instructions to candidates
- All answers must be written in the Question Booklet.
- **Do not** write any answers on the Source Documents.

Document A

OPESD
Organisation for Post-Exam Safe Drivers

Just passing your driving test is no longer enough. Driving instructors are now recommending that motorists should take a course of post-exam driving lessons to improve their driving skills. The Organisation for Post-Exam Safe Drivers (OPESD) is offering courses, ranging from a day to two weeks, that can help drivers feel much safer on the roads. All OPESD courses aim to:

- Make drivers more aware of hazards on the road, like snow and black ice, and how they can avoid potential accidents.

- Make sure that drivers know the correct procedures to follow if an accident does happen or is encountered on the road.

- Make the country's roads a safer place for both drivers and other road users.

- Help drivers to be confident in a variety of different road conditions, such as at night, on the motorway, on country lanes and in cities.

- Introduce more advanced driving techniques that aren't required to pass the standard driving test.

- Encourage drivers to become more economical.*

*Economical driving reduces wear and tear on vehicles. It is important because it not only lowers the chance of an accident occurring, but also helps lower fuel consumption, which reduces the cost of motoring.

With around 40 million roadworthy vehicles in the UK, making sure you can drive safely and confidently has never been more important. Don't delay — book your course today!

OPESD are currently offering some spectacular deals on their driving courses:

Option 1

If you have just passed your test, we recommend a two-week intensive course to boost your confidence and enhance your road safety skills — our two-week course has been reduced from £500 to £390. It's a priceless investment for years of safety!

Option 2

If you have been driving for a few months or more, but still want to improve with a fairly quick booster, the weekend course would be a great way to improve your road safety knowledge — it's also a bargain at £150 for the entire 10-hour course.

Option 3

At OPESD, we think that there's always more to learn. As a result, we have introduced new, one-day sessions for confident drivers who have been on the roads for years. These can help to quickly refresh road skills and keep you up-to-date with the latest advancements in road safety — all for just £50.

Get in touch to book your course at an unbeatable price!

Document B

Safe Driving

| Home | Safe Driving | Cars | Motorcycles | Pedestrians | Road Signs | Contact Us |

Learning to drive is a thrilling experience. Once you've passed your test, though, it's essential that you continue to drive carefully to keep yourself and other road users safe. The following advice is all you need to make sure you stay out of danger.

Keeping things running

It's not just about how you drive — what you drive is important too. You'll need to make sure your vehicle is roadworthy. Do this by checking your oil and keeping it topped up to the correct level. You should check the level of your windscreen washer fluid and fill your washer bottle up before long journeys. Furthermore, if you notice anything different about your car, such as noises you've not heard before, get it checked at a garage.

Getting a grip

You should also check the tread depth on your tyres is deep enough — the legal minimum tread depth in the UK is 1.6 mm across 75% of the tyre. If the tread on your tyres is getting close to this value, you'll need to get new ones to make sure you stay safe — old and worn tyres mean that your car takes much longer to come to a complete stop.

Fighting tiredness

You need to take into account your physical and mental state when driving anywhere. Tiredness reduces concentration, so if you're shattered, you won't be safe to drive and should rest until you feel more alert. Some prescription medicines can make you feel a bit groggy, so check the packaging before driving. Make sure you stop for a rest every few hours on long journeys to revive your energy levels.

Staying on the straight and narrow

At times, it seems like there's an overwhelming number of rules of the road and many people think they need only learn the most important ones. However, they are vital for keeping you and the people around you safe. You ought to keep up-to-date with the wealth of information in the Highway Code. You can find the Highway Code and refresher tests online for free.

And remember, speed restrictions and road signs are put in place for a reason, and you should always obey them — if you are stopped by a police officer, "I didn't see the sign!" isn't an acceptable excuse.

Keep these things in mind, and you should have no trouble on the roads.

BLANK PAGE

Candidate Surname	Candidate Forename(s)

Date	Candidate Signature

Functional Skills

English   Level 2

Reading

Road Safety

Question Booklet

Time allowed: 1 hour

You **may** use a dictionary.

Information for candidates
- Answer **all questions** in the spaces provided.
- There are **30 marks** available for this paper.
- The marks available for each question are given in brackets.

Instructions to candidates
- Use **black or blue ink** to write your answers.
- Write your name and the date in the spaces provided above.
- Read each question carefully before you start answering it.
- You do not need to write in full sentences.
- You will not be marked on spelling, punctuation or grammar.

Total Marks

Answer every question. Write your answers in the spaces provided.

Section A

You'll need to read Document A to answer Questions 1 to 6.

1 What is the **main** purpose of Document A? Tick **one** box

    A To inform people about how they can become a better driver ☐

    B To argue that driving tests should be made much harder ☐

    C To persuade people to pay for additional driving lessons ☐

    D To encourage people to drive more economically ☐

[1 mark]

2 What style of writing is used in the phrase 'improve with a fairly quick booster'? Tick **one** box.

    A conversational ☐

    B instructive ☐

    C humorous ☐

    D argumentative ☐

[1 mark]

3 Which of the following titles would be the most suitable for Document A? Tick **one** box.

    A Make the roads a safer place ☐

    B Improve your driving with OPESD ☐

    C Number of cars nears 40 million ☐

    D Hazard awareness must be improved ☐

[1 mark]

4 Document A doesn't mention how to get in touch with OPESD.

    What else is **not** included in the document that you might
    expect to find on an advert for educational courses?

    ....

    ....

[2 marks]

5   Document A contains both facts and opinions.

Give **two facts** and **two opinions** from Document A.

Fact 1 ....

....

Fact 2 ....

....

Opinion 1 ....

....

Opinion 2 ....

....

[4 marks]

6   Give **two** examples of persuasive language from Document A.

For each example, give a **different** effect this persuasive language has on the reader.

Example 1 ....

....

Effect 1 ....

....

Example 2 ....

....

Effect 2 ....

....

[4 marks]

Section B

You'll need to read Document B to answer Questions 7 to 14.

7 Document B is divided up by subheadings.

What is the subheading for the section about the importance of checking your tyres?
Tick **one** box.

A Keeping things running ☐

B Getting a grip ☐

C Fighting tiredness ☐

D Staying on the straight and narrow ☐

[1 mark]

8 Which statement below **best** sums up what Document B says about the rules of the road?
Tick **one** box.

A There are lots of rules of the road. ☐

B You should keep up-to-date using online tests. ☐

C They are an important part of keeping people safe. ☐

D You only need to learn the most important rules. ☐

[1 mark]

9 Document B tells you about how being tired can affect your concentration and driving ability.

Which **two** more informal words does Document B use instead of 'tired'?

....

....

[2 marks]

10 The writer of Document B uses both facts and opinions.

Give **one** opinion from Document B.

....

....

[1 mark]

11 Document B uses direct address throughout.

Give **two** effects that this use of direct address has on readers.

....

....

....

....

[2 marks]

12 The writer of Document B thinks that you shouldn't drive while tired.

Give **two** quotations that suggest this.

....

....

....

....

[2 marks]

13 Your friend wants to know more about road signs. Which **two** features used in Document B could help your friend learn more about them?

....

....

[2 marks]

14 What are the **two** main purposes of Document B? Tick **two** boxes.

    A To advertise ☐   **D** To entertain ☐

    B To educate ☐   **E** To instruct ☐

    C To argue ☐   **F** To discuss ☐

Section C

You'll need to read both documents to answer Question 15.

15 Document A and Document B give different ideas about how to be safe on the road.

Using **one** example from **each** document, compare how these ideas differ.

....

....

....

....

....

Using **one** example from **each** document, show a similarity or difference in how these ideas are **conveyed** to the reader.

....

....

....

....

....

[4 marks]

Total for paper = 30 marks

BLANK PAGE

Knowing Your Audience and Purpose

Audience and purpose are important

1) An **audience** is the **person or people** who read a text.

2) You need to know who your **audience** is so you can decide whether your writing should be **formal** or **informal**.

> For more on formal and informal writing, see p.28.

3) You might see a text's **level of formality** referred to as its **register**.

4) The **purpose** of a text is the **reason** it is written. For example, to **explain** or **persuade**.

Find out who you are writing for and why

In the writing test, use the question to tell you **who** the text is for and **why** you are writing it.

The audience is your friend.

Write an email to your friend persuading them to volunteer at a youth centre.

The purpose is to persuade your friend to volunteer at a youth centre.

Use the right writing style

Make sure your **writing style** is **suitable** for the **audience** and the **purpose**.

The audience is the guests.   The purpose is to tell them about the hotel.

Write a leaflet for new guests telling them what is on offer at your hotel.

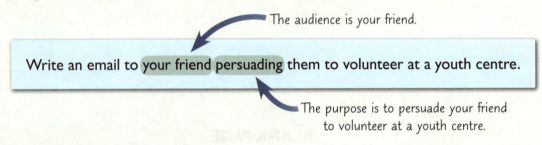

The writing would be formal.

Our hotel has lots to offer. Our facilities include a heated outdoor swimming pool and satellite TV. We also provide delicious breakfasts.

The audience is your friend.   The purpose is to persuade him to sponsor you.

Write an email to your friend persuading him to sponsor you.

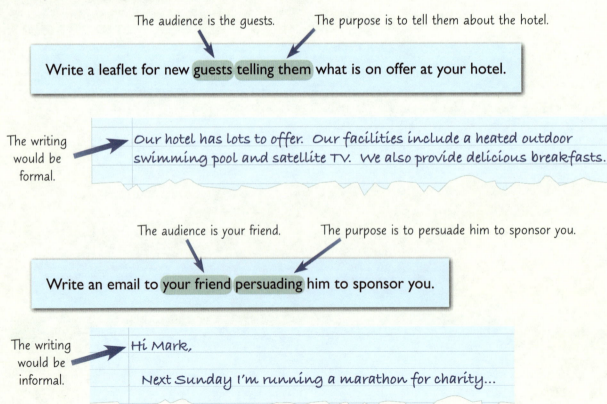

The writing would be informal.

Hi Mark,

Next Sunday I'm running a marathon for charity...

Practice Questions

1) Write down the audience and purpose for each of these writing tasks.

   a) Write a leaflet for tourists explaining what there is to do in your town.

   Audience ....

   Purpose ....

   b) Write an email to your council complaining about the lack of recycling facilities in your area.

   Audience ....

   Purpose ....

   c) Write a letter applying for volunteer work in a charity shop.

   Audience ....

   Purpose ....

   d) Write a letter to your boss persuading them to give you flexible working hours.

   Audience ....

   Purpose ....

   e) Write an article for a newspaper advising people on how to save money.

   Audience ....

   Purpose ....

2) Formal writing is for people you don't know, or for work and other professional situations. Informal writing is for people you know well.

   What type of writing style would you use for these writing tasks? Circle 'Formal' or 'Informal'.

   a) A letter to a neighbour asking them to feed your cat   Formal / Informal

   b) An email to a supermarket complaining about mouldy food   Formal / Informal

   c) A film review for your local newspaper   Formal / Informal

   d) An email to a family friend about a recent holiday   Formal / Informal

   e) A blog post for your college's website about a charity event. Formal / Informal

Planning Your Answer

Make a plan before you start writing

1) Planning your answer will help you put your ideas **in order**.

2) A plan **doesn't** need to be in full sentences. Just write down your **key** ideas to **save time**.

3) Make sure you **only** write down points that **answer the question**.

4) You will be given **space** to plan your answer in the test, but it **won't** be **marked**.

5) You can also use this planning space to do a **first draft** if you need to.

Use notes to write your plan

1) Work out the **audience** and **purpose** and whether you should be **formal** or **informal**.

2) Write down the **points** you want to include.

3) **Organise** your points so that the **most important** ideas come **first**.

4) If you're given **bullet points** in the question, you could include them in your plan.

The audience is the council.   The purpose is to inform about the problems in your town.

Write an email to your council telling them about problems in your town.

Most important point comes first.

Audience: council (formal)   Purpose: inform
1) Potholes in road — makes driving dangerous
2) Not enough street lighting — unsafe at night
3) Littering on pavements — attracts rats

How to plan letters and emails

1) Work out who the audience is to decide if your writing should be **formal** or **informal**.

2) This will help you decide which **greeting** and **ending** to use (see page 68).

3) Your first paragraph should tell the reader **why** you are writing to them.

4) The main body of the letter or email should **develop** your ideas and give more **detail**.

5) The last paragraph should tell the reader what **action** you want them to take.

Planning Your Answer

How to plan an article

Work out your **purpose** and **audience**.
Think about **where** the article will be printed.

> Blog posts are similar to articles, but instead of being printed in a newspaper they are published online.

> Write an article for a local newspaper discussing plans for a new youth centre.

The audience for the article is local people.

Start with the main facts. What it is, where it is and when construction is due to start.

> Audience: newspaper readers (formal) Purpose: to discuss
> 1) Youth centre / Herman Road / building begins in April
> 2) Arguments for the youth centre
> 3) Arguments against the youth centre

Then go into detail about the subject. If there are two sides to an argument, make sure you discuss both.

How to plan a report

The purpose of a report is to **give information**. It needs to be **clear** and **accurate**.

> You are a lifeguard at a swimming pool. A swimmer slipped on the poolside. The Safety Officer has asked you to write a report about what happened.

Use formal language for reports.

> Injury: broken wrist, bruised ribs
> Cause: water on poolside
> Solution: safety signs, more frequent cleaning

Divide the information clearly into sections.

How to plan a forum response or a review

1) The purpose of these text types is to **give** your **opinion** and **argue** a point of view.

2) Forum responses and reviews can also be used to **explain** something.

3) Your **first point** should clearly explain your main argument.

4) You'll get better marks if your **argument** is **balanced**.

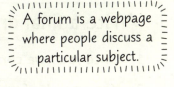

> A forum is a webpage where people discuss a particular subject.

5) So remember to include a point or two from the **other side** of the argument.

6) The rest of your points should **back up** your **argument**. Use P.E.E.

7) Use **persuasive language** to convince people of your point of view.

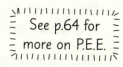

> See p.64 for more on P.E.E.

Writing and Checking Your Answer

Use your plan to write your answer

1) Put the ideas in your plan into **full sentences**.

2) Use the same **order** and **structure** you decided on in your plan.

3) Make sure your writing style is right for your **audience** and **purpose**.

Improve your writing by checking it

Make sure you leave enough time to read through your answer.

1) Read over your answer carefully and **make improvements**.

2) Don't **repeat** yourself. Make each point **once** and take out anything you **don't need**.

3) Check that your **spelling**, **punctuation** and **grammar** are correct.

Make sure your corrections are neat

1) **Cross out** any **mistakes** neatly and **write** any corrections **above** them.

breakfast
The hotel serves ~~brekfast~~ from 7 am until 10 am.

If you've made a mistake, cross it out and clearly rewrite the whole word above it.

2) Draw two lines (*II*) to show where a **new paragraph** should start.

...great for children. **II** Secondly, there is a zoo nearby.

A double strike shows that you want a new paragraph to start here.

3) Use the symbol ∧ below the line to **add** in one word, or a **star** to **add** in **more than one**.

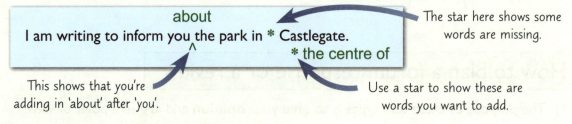

about
I am writing to inform you ∧ the park in * Castlegate.
                                          * the centre of

The star here shows some words are missing.

This shows that you're adding in 'about' after 'you'.

Use a star to show these are words you want to add.

Write a final draft if you have time

1) Once you have **corrected** your answer, you might want to write out a **final draft**.

2) **Keep track** of the **time** you have left. You might not have time for a final draft in the test.

3) Don't panic if you don't have time — just make sure that any **corrections** you've written are **clear enough** for the examiner to understand.

4) Drafting is often used in more **formal situations**, like when you're writing a **report** at work.

Practice Question

1) Read the following writing task and the example plan for an answer.

> You are planning a day out at a theme park.
> Write an email to your friends encouraging them to come with you.

> <u>Audience:</u> your friends (informal) <u>Purpose:</u> persuade / inform
>
> <u>Details</u>
> • What: Day out at a theme park
> • When: May 22nd — leave at 8 am, arrive by 10 am
> • Where: Talltown Towers — directions / take train to Uxley
>
> <u>Anything else</u>
> • Bring waterproofs — you will get wet on some rides
> • Other friends welcome
> • Half-price tickets if you book online

Remember to start a new paragraph every time you talk about a new bullet point.

Turn this plan into a full answer. Make improvements and add details as you write.

....

....

....

....

....

....

....

....

....

....

....

....

....

Using Paragraphs

Paragraphs make your writing easier to read

1) A paragraph is a **group of sentences**.

2) These sentences talk about the **same thing** or **follow on** from each other.

Divide your plan into paragraphs

1) You could give each **point** in your plan its own **paragraph**.

2) Start with an **introduction** paragraph. It should **summarise** what your answer is about.

3) Make your last paragraph a **conclusion**. It should **sum up** your main point.

Use paragraphs to show when something changes

1) Start a new paragraph when you talk about a different **topic**, **person**, **place** or **time**.

2) To show a new paragraph, start a new line and leave a **space** at the beginning.

Leave a space to show it's a new paragraph.

Different person.

Start a new paragraph on a new line.

Different place.

> Surveys suggest that Ulrow shoppers are leaving Christmas shopping later each year.
>
> Bill Todd, a local shop-owner, said that last year the busiest day in the festive period was Christmas Eve.
>
> In Barston, the trend is very different. Similar surveys show that the week running up to Christmas is their quietest.

3) If you are writing **online**, you often leave a **whole line** blank between each paragraph.

4) You will **lose marks** if your writing isn't in paragraphs.

Your paragraphs should usually be longer than one sentence.

Use P.E.E. to develop your points

P.E.E. stands for **Point, Example, Explanation**. It helps to **structure** your paragraphs.

Make your point first.

Give an example of your point.

> Using an officially registered gas engineer is important. Each year, hundreds of people are hospitalised because of unsafe gas work. Nearly all of these incidents were caused by unregistered gas engineers not doing a proper job.

Explain how the example backs up your point.

Practice Question

1) Read this piece of writing about coffee shops.
   Rewrite it underneath with new paragraphs in the correct places.

New coffee shops are opening every day in the UK. It is thought that the number of coffee shops will increase by 50% in just a few years. Some people believe that the British interest in coffee began in 1978, when the first coffee shops opened in London. When it became clear that these shops were making a lot of money, more and more began appearing all over the country. Last year, the coffee shop industry grew by around 8%, meaning that coffee shops are now worth £10 billion to the UK economy. However, this growth may not continue. Research suggests that the number of coffee shops could reach a limit within the next few years.

....

....

....

....

....

....

....

....

....

....

....

....

....

....

....

....

Writing Emails

You need to be able to write different text types

1) In the writing test, you could be asked to write **two** different **text types**.

2) Text types are just different ways of **presenting information**, like an **email** or a **report**.

3) You will get **marks** for how you **set out** your text.

4) For example, you'll get marks for setting out a **letter** correctly.

5) But don't worry about writing in **columns** or adding **pictures**.

6) Remember it's a writing test, so focus on the **content** and the **structure** of your answer.

Make sure the style of your email is right for the audience

1) When you email a **company** or **someone important**, use **formal** language.

2) You should also use **formal** language if you're emailing someone you **don't know**.

3) Emails to **family** and **friends** can be more **informal**.

Lay out emails correctly

Make sure you include all the **right information**.

EXAMPLE:

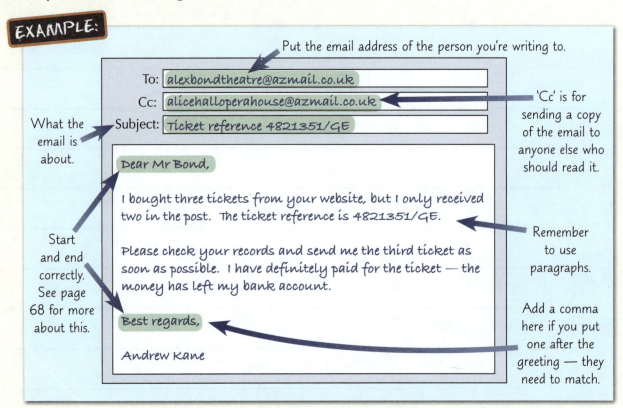

Put the email address of the person you're writing to.

To: alexbondtheatre@azmail.co.uk

Cc: alicehalloperahouse@azmail.co.uk

'Cc' is for sending a copy of the email to anyone else who should read it.

What the email is about.

Subject: Ticket reference 4821351/GE

Dear Mr Bond,

I bought three tickets from your website, but I only received two in the post. The ticket reference is 4821351/GE.

Please check your records and send me the third ticket as soon as possible. I have definitely paid for the ticket — the money has left my bank account.

Remember to use paragraphs.

Start and end correctly. See page 68 for more about this.

Best regards,

Andrew Kane

Add a comma here if you put one after the greeting — they need to match.

Practice Question

1) Read this email from a co-worker about the office Christmas party.

	From:	harry.coates@azmail.co.uk
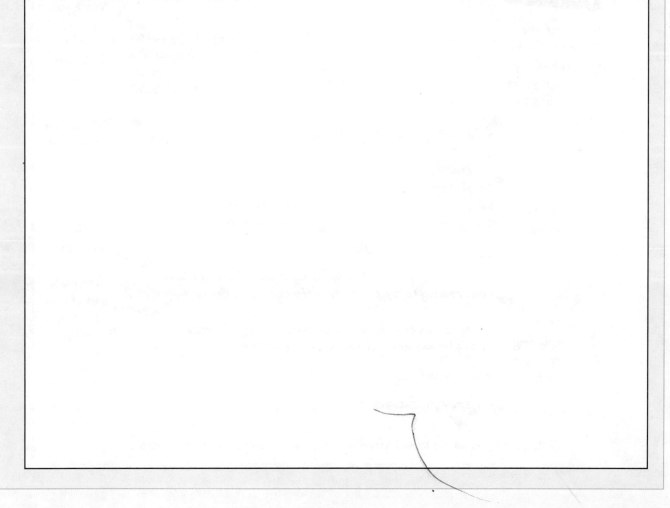	To:	Office_All
Reply	Subject:	Christmas party

Hello

I'm organising the Christmas party this year, and I'm looking for some help to put it together. We're holding the party at the Armadillo Hotel on Wednesday 21st December. It would be great if a few of you could help me put up some decorations, book the DJ and organise the food.

Let me know if you'd like to help out. Any ideas or suggestions for the party would be great.

Cheers
Harry

You need to write a short reply which tells Harry that you would like to help organise the party and how you would like to help out. You should also include any suggestions you have for the party.

Use the space below to plan your answer. Write your answer on a separate piece of paper. Make sure your spelling, punctuation and grammar are correct.

Writing Letters

Formal letters are for people you don't know

1) Start with a **formal greeting**. For example, 'Dear Mr Jones' or 'Dear Sir / Madam'.

2) **End** with 'Yours sincerely' if you know their name, or 'Yours faithfully' if you don't.

3) Avoid **slang**, **exclamation marks** and **abbreviations**.

Informal letters are for people you know well

1) Start with the **name** of who you're sending it to.

2) **End** with something like '**Best wishes**' or '**See you soon**'.

3) You can be more **chatty**, but make sure your spelling and grammar are correct.

Follow the rules for writing letters

There are some things that all **letters** need.

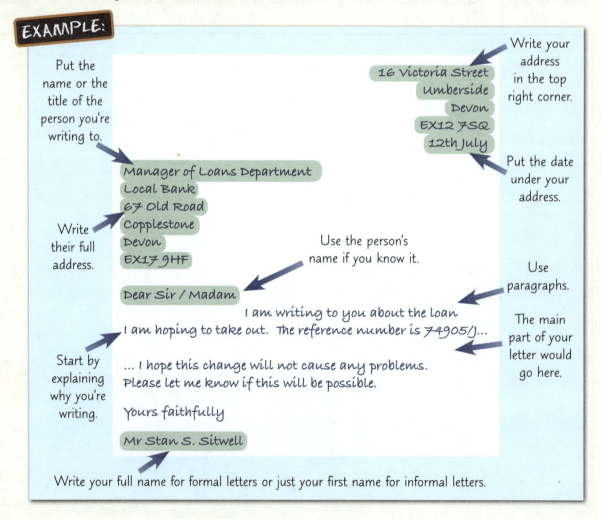

EXAMPLE:

Put the name or the title of the person you're writing to.

Write their full address.

Start by explaining why you're writing.

16 Victoria Street
Umberside
Devon
EX12 7SQ
12th July

Write your address in the top right corner.

Put the date under your address.

Manager of Loans Department
Local Bank
67 Old Road
Copplestone
Devon
EX17 9HF

Use the person's name if you know it.

Dear Sir / Madam

I am writing to you about the loan I am hoping to take out. The reference number is 74905/...

... I hope this change will not cause any problems. Please let me know if this will be possible.

Yours faithfully

Mr Stan S. Sitwell

Use paragraphs.

The main part of your letter would go here.

Write your full name for formal letters or just your first name for informal letters.

Practice Question

1) You see the advert below.

> Mitterdon Community Centre is a local centre where young people can learn new skills, play sports and engage in team-bonding exercises in a safe environment. We are looking for someone to volunteer to run a sports or craft programme. Please contact Mrs Susan Holt to apply. The address is: Mitterdon Community Centre, 19 Church Street, Stockport, SK8 7DN. Remember to include any relevant experience you might have and a brief explanation of why you would be the right person for the role.

Write a letter to volunteer for the organisation described above. Think about:

- the layout and tone of the letter

- why you want to volunteer for this organisation

- suggestions for activities you could run

Use the space below to plan your answer. Write your answer on a separate piece of paper. Make sure your spelling, punctuation and grammar are correct.

Writing Articles

Articles appear in newspapers or magazines

1) Articles are usually **formal** texts which **explain** something to the reader.

2) When writing an article, you may want to **persuade** the reader to **agree** with your **point of view**.

3) Use **facts** and **figures** to **provide information** and to **support** your **opinion**.

Articles often include specialist words

1) Some words are only used to talk about **particular subjects**.

2) These are known as **specialist words**.

3) You might use words like '**shipment**' or '**vehicle**' to talk about **transport**.

4) If you were writing a **newspaper article**, you might use words like '**eyewitness**' or '**statistics**'.

Turn to p.112 for tips on spelling specialist words.

Think about the structure of your article

An answer to an **article question** might look like this.

EXAMPLE:

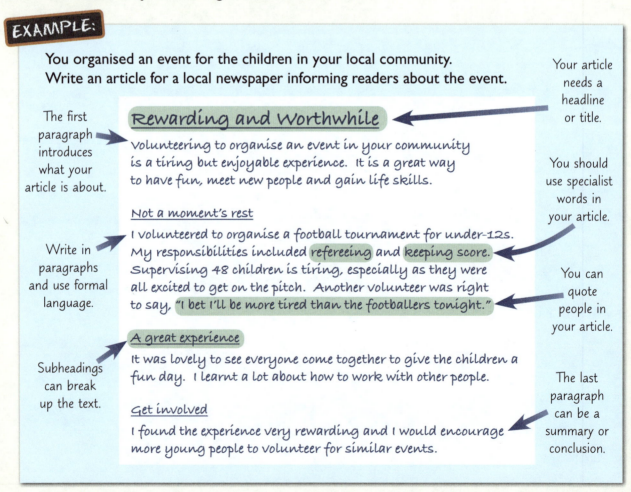

You organised an event for the children in your local community.
Write an article for a local newspaper informing readers about the event.

The first paragraph introduces what your article is about.

Rewarding and Worthwhile

Volunteering to organise an event in your community is a tiring but enjoyable experience. It is a great way to have fun, meet new people and gain life skills.

Your article needs a headline or title.

You should use specialist words in your article.

Write in paragraphs and use formal language.

Not a moment's rest

I volunteered to organise a football tournament for under-12s. My responsibilities included refereeing and keeping score. Supervising 48 children is tiring, especially as they were all excited to get on the pitch. Another volunteer was right to say, "I bet I'll be more tired than the footballers tonight."

You can quote people in your article.

Subheadings can break up the text.

A great experience

It was lovely to see everyone come together to give the children a fun day. I learnt a lot about how to work with other people.

Get involved

I found the experience very rewarding and I would encourage more young people to volunteer for similar events.

The last paragraph can be a summary or conclusion.

Practice Question

1) You went to the event below.

> Charity Dinner for the Jane Bauer Foundation
>
> On Saturday 21st September, the Jane Bauer Foundation held a charity dinner in order to raise money for the local hospital. The dinner included an auction, a speech by the head of the Foundation (Mr James Johnson) and a raffle with a selection of great prizes. The event raised far more than its target of £2,500.

Write a newspaper article about the event. Think about:

• the layout and tone of your article

• the reason for the charity dinner

• what happened at the event

Use the space below to plan your answer. Write your answer on a separate piece of paper. Make sure your spelling, punctuation and grammar are correct.

Writing Reports

Reports provide information

1) Reports give the reader **information** and **recommendations** about something.

2) They need to be **formal** and **informative**.

Reports summarise an issue

1) Write an **introduction** for your report to **explain** the issue you're writing about.

2) The main part of your report will **summarise** the **important points** about the issue.

3) In your **conclusion**, you'll give your **advice** or **opinion** about the issue.

Reports should be balanced

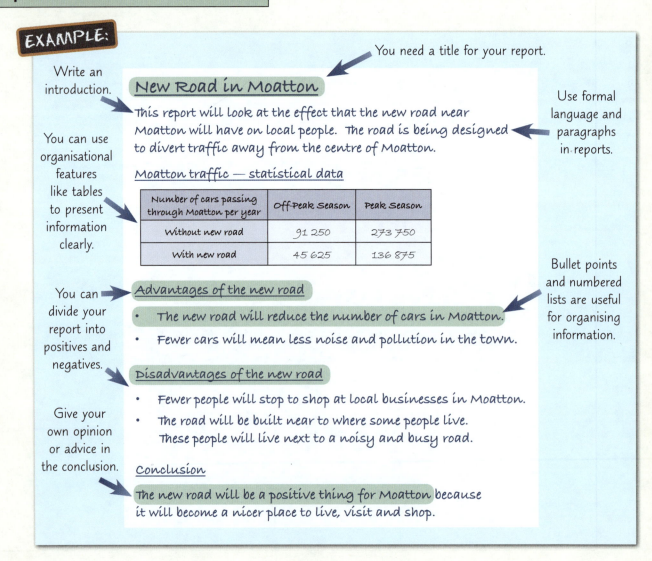

EXAMPLE:

You need a title for your report.

Write an introduction.

New Road in Moatton

This report will look at the effect that the new road near Moatton will have on local people. The road is being designed to divert traffic away from the centre of Moatton.

Use formal language and paragraphs in reports.

You can use organisational features like tables to present information clearly.

Moatton traffic — statistical data

Number of cars passing through Moatton per year	Off-Peak Season	Peak Season
Without new road	91 250	273 750
With new road	45 625	136 875

You can divide your report into positives and negatives.

Advantages of the new road

- The new road will reduce the number of cars in Moatton.
- Fewer cars will mean less noise and pollution in the town.

Bullet points and numbered lists are useful for organising information.

Disadvantages of the new road

- Fewer people will stop to shop at local businesses in Moatton.
- The road will be built near to where some people live. These people will live next to a noisy and busy road.

Give your own opinion or advice in the conclusion.

Conclusion

The new road will be a positive thing for Moatton because it will become a nicer place to live, visit and shop.

Practice Question

1) Read the article below.

Burnham Community Theatre to Close

It was announced today that Burnham Community Theatre will close to make way for a new car park in the town centre. The Community Theatre, which provides a variety of community activities during the week, has been an important part of Burnham for 15 years. The theatre holds a different class or activity every day of the week, and its Christmas pantomime sells out every year. Burnham's theatre-goers will now have to travel up to 50 miles to see a play. Some residents are in favour of the new car park because it will create 460 parking spaces and will help to reduce parking problems in Burnham. Businesses and shops in the town centre believe that the new car park will help attract shoppers to the area and boost their sales.

Community Theatre Weekly Schedule	
Day	Event
Monday	First aid class
Tuesday	Choir practice
Wednesday	Dance class
Thursday	Karate class
Friday	Aerobics class
Saturday	Drama class
Sunday	Yoga class

Write a report about how the council's plans might affect Burnham. Think about:

• the positives of the new car park

• the negatives of the Community Theatre closing

• your opinion about the change

Use the space below to plan your answer. Write your answer on a separate piece of paper. Make sure your spelling, punctuation and grammar are correct.

Writing Leaflets

Leaflets can have different purposes

1) Leaflets often provide **information** about something. For example, buying a house.

2) Leaflets can also **persuade** a reader to do something. For example, donate blood.

Know who your audience is

1) You need to make sure the **language** and **style** used in the leaflet **suits** its **audience**.

2) You might use **formal** and **serious language** for a leaflet about fire hazards at home.

3) You might use **chatty** language for a leaflet **persuading** readers to visit a museum.

The information in a leaflet needs to be laid out clearly

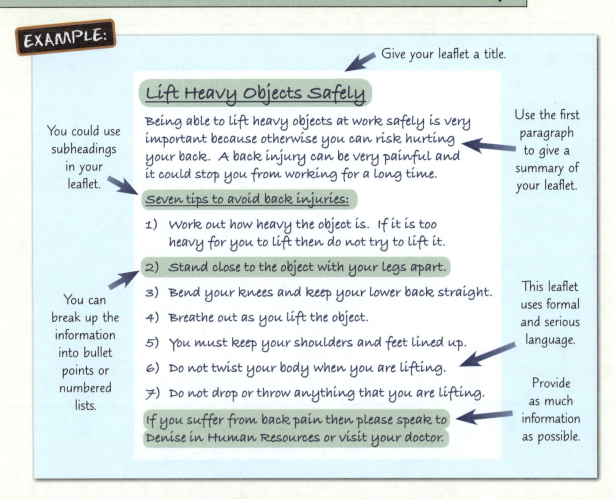

EXAMPLE:

Give your leaflet a title.

Lift Heavy Objects Safely

Being able to lift heavy objects at work safely is very important because otherwise you can risk hurting your back. A back injury can be very painful and it could stop you from working for a long time.

You could use subheadings in your leaflet.

Use the first paragraph to give a summary of your leaflet.

Seven tips to avoid back injuries:

1) Work out how heavy the object is. If it is too heavy for you to lift then do not try to lift it.

2) Stand close to the object with your legs apart.

3) Bend your knees and keep your lower back straight.

4) Breathe out as you lift the object.

5) You must keep your shoulders and feet lined up.

6) Do not twist your body when you are lifting.

7) Do not drop or throw anything that you are lifting.

If you suffer from back pain then please speak to Denise in Human Resources or visit your doctor.

You can break up the information into bullet points or numbered lists.

This leaflet uses formal and serious language.

Provide as much information as possible.

Practice Question

1) You receive the email below from someone you work with.

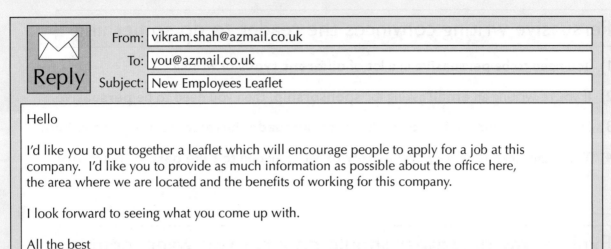

From: vikram.shah@azmail.co.uk
To: you@azmail.co.uk
Subject: New Employees Leaflet

Hello

I'd like you to put together a leaflet which will encourage people to apply for a job at this company. I'd like you to provide as much information as possible about the office here, the area where we are located and the benefits of working for this company.

I look forward to seeing what you come up with.

All the best
Vikram

Write a leaflet which:

- tells people what the company you work for is like

- gives information about the area in which your company is located

- persuades people to apply for a job at your company

Use the space below to plan your answer. Write your answer on a separate piece of paper. Make sure your spelling, punctuation and grammar are correct.

Writing Persuasively

Persuasive writing convinces the reader to do something

1) You need to be **persuasive** in a lot of **different types** of writing.

2) If you're writing an **email** asking for **sponsorship**, then you need to be **persuasive**.

3) In a **letter** of **complaint** you might try to **persuade** the reader to give you a **refund**.

4) You might need to write **persuasively** to get someone to **take part** in an **activity**.

Explain why the reader should do what you want them to

To be persuasive you need to **give reasons why** someone should do something.

> You should donate £5 a month to the 'Build a Well' foundation because your money will provide clean and safe water to hundreds of people.

This gives the reader a reason why they should donate.

Persuasive writing makes the reader feel something

1) Use **descriptive words** in persuasive writing.

2) These descriptive words can make the reader **feel** a **certain emotion**.

These words make the reader feel angry.

> These animals are forced to live in appalling conditions. Their cruel owners don't feed them properly and keep them in tiny cages. You can put a stop to this.

3) Using words like '**you**' and '**your**' is called **direct address** — it makes a text **more persuasive**.

4) This is because it sounds like you are **talking directly** to the **reader**.

5) Words like '**we**' and '**our**' have a similar effect.

These words make the reader feel involved.

> We need to take action and reduce the amount of single-use plastics we throw away. Even by making small lifestyle changes, like using paper straws or reusable bottles, we can have a real impact on tackling the current environmental crisis.

Practice Question

1) You want to enter the competition below.

A Deserved Break

Here at Relax Holidays, we're giving away a free seven-day holiday to Barbados to whoever we think really deserves a break. So, if you're someone who works really hard and has no time to relax, or someone who has gone through a tough patch and needs to get away from it all, get in touch. Write us a short letter, and give us plenty of reasons why you think you deserve a break. Who knows, you might get that break you deserve.

Contact us at: Relax Holidays, 4 Mill Street, Holloway, London, N7 7DE

Write a letter to persuade the staff at Relax Holidays to award you the free holiday.
Remember to:

• think about the layout and tone of your letter

• give reasons why you should be chosen

Use the space below to plan your answer. Write your answer on a separate piece of paper. Make sure your spelling, punctuation and grammar are correct.

Writing About Your Opinions

Sometimes you'll need to give your opinion

1) You may be asked if you **agree** or **disagree** with something.

2) This means you need to give **your own opinion**.

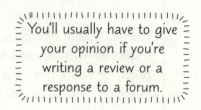

You'll usually have to give your opinion if you're writing a review or a response to a forum.

Give evidence to support your opinions

1) Your opinion **can't** be **right** or **wrong**.

2) However, you have to **back up** your opinion with **evidence**.

> Parents, not schools, should be responsible for teaching their children to read. Children learn more quickly when they are taught one-to-one.

This is the writer's opinion.

This is the evidence to support the writer's opinion.

3) Your opinion will sound **more convincing** if it's supported by **evidence**.

You might find it difficult to pick your opinion

1) It's fine to **argue both sides** of an argument.

2) You should try to reach a **conclusion** in your answer though.

> I think that the new supermarket will bring jobs to the area and cheaper prices for food. Unfortunately, it will also bring more traffic, and it will force local businesses to close. As a result, I am against the new supermarket, because it will bring more negatives than positives to the area.

This is one opinion. It's in favour of the new supermarket.

This is another opinion. It's opposed to the new supermarket.

Here the writer has chosen one opinion over the other.

3) Even if you **disagree** with someone, your language should be **polite** and **respectful**.

Practice Question

1) You read the comments below on an internet forum.

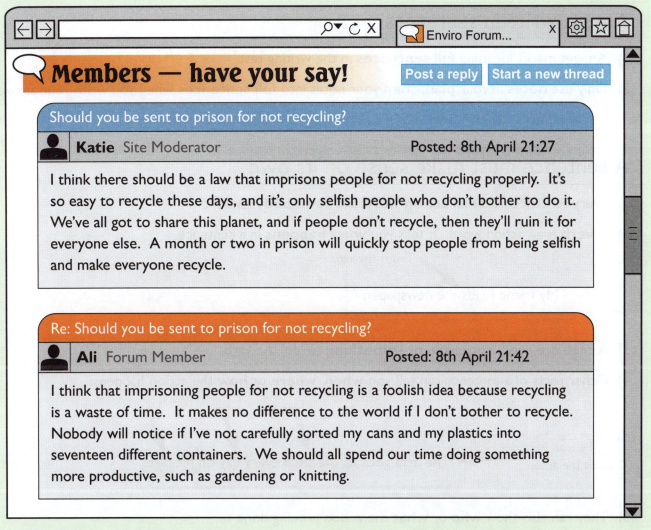

Write your own comment for the Enviro Forum giving your views about whether people should be sent to prison for not recycling. Do not just repeat what has already been said — try to come up with your own ideas. Use the space below to plan your answer. Make sure your spelling, punctuation and grammar are correct.

Using Sentences

Always write in sentences

1) You get marks for using **full sentences** in the writing test.

2) Only use **notes** in your **plan**. Turn your notes into **full sentences** when you write your answer.

A sentence must make sense on its own

1) Every sentence needs an **action word** and **somebody** to do it.

2) A **verb** is an action word. It tells you **what happens** in a sentence.

This is the verb.

My friend reads the newspaper.

3) A sentence needs **someone** or **something** to 'do' the verb.

4) Other parts of a sentence can tell you **when**, **where** or **how** the action happens.

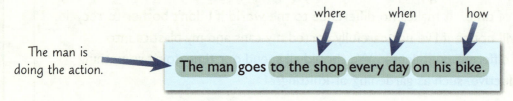

where   when   how

The man is doing the action.

The man goes to the shop every day on his bike.

5) They can also show **who** or **what** the action is being done to.

The visiting was 'done' to the neighbour.

I visited my neighbour.

Make sure your sentences are straight to the point

1) Make sure your sentences aren't **too long** or **confusing**.

2) If a sentence is too long, consider **splitting** it into **two shorter sentences**.

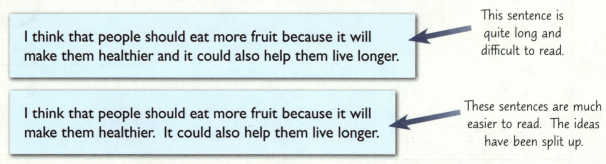

I think that people should eat more fruit because it will make them healthier and it could also help them live longer.

This sentence is quite long and difficult to read.

I think that people should eat more fruit because it will make them healthier. It could also help them live longer.

These sentences are much easier to read. The ideas have been split up.

Using Sentences

Use the correct articles to be specific or general

1) Articles are the words 'a', 'an' and 'the'. They go before nouns.

2) 'A' and 'an' are used for **general** things:

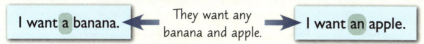

I want a banana. ← They want any banana and apple. → I want an apple.

3) 'The' is used for **specific** things:

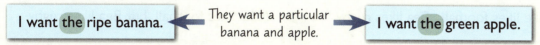

I want the ripe banana. ← They want a particular banana and apple. → I want the green apple.

You use 'an' and 'a' at different times

1) Use '**an**' when the **next word** starts with a **vowel sound** — e.g. 'an apple' or 'an orange'.

2) Use '**a**' when the **next word** starts with a **consonant sound** — e.g. 'a banana' or 'a lime'.

3) Be careful — some words are **spelt** with one letter but **sound** like another.

4) For example, 'universe' sounds like 'you-niverse', so you use '**a**' instead of '**an**'.

Practice Questions

1) Underline the **verb** in each sentence.

    a) We arrived at the restaurant early.   b) Everyone likes chocolate milkshakes.

2) Underline **who** or **what** is doing the action in each sentence.

    a) Rabbits often eat garden plants.   b) The supermarket is open all day.

3) Underline **when** the action happens in each sentence.

    a) He went to work early.   b) She goes swimming on Tuesdays.

4) Underline **where** the action happens in each sentence.

    a) We often go to an Italian restaurant. b) I visited the art gallery last week.

5) Choose 'a' or 'an' to complete these sentences.

    a) There was .... unusual smell in the kitchen.

    b) I'm looking for .... new hairdresser.

    c) There's .... ant in my tea.

    d) They gave the restaurant .... one-star review.

    e) He will be ready in .... hour.

Using Joining Words to Add Detail

Joining words develop your writing

1) **Joining words connect** parts of sentences **together**.

2) You can use these words to join two **separate sentences** together:

> for   and   nor   but   or   yet   so

> Mike likes football. Bea likes rugby. ➡️ Mike likes football, **but** Bea likes rugby.

3) You can use these words to join the **main part** of a sentence to a **less important** part:

> until   although   if   because   while   after

> I enjoy shopping **because I like clothes.** ⬅ 'because I like clothes' is just an extra detail and doesn't make sense on its own.

4) Using joining words in sentences will make your writing **more interesting**.

5) This will help you **pick up marks** in your writing test.

6) Don't **overuse** joining words — too many can make your sentences long and difficult to follow.

'And', 'because' and 'so' add another point

Use '**and**', '**because**' or '**so**' to add **more detail** to a sentence.

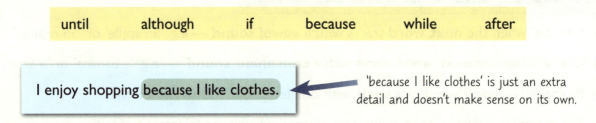

> Amy is happy **because** she won the lottery.

> Jake is getting fit, **so** he goes jogging every night.

'because' and 'so' introduce explanations.

'But' and 'or' disagree with a point

1) Use '**but**' to **disagree** with something that's just been said.

> Oliver usually has toast for breakfast, **but** today he had cereal.

2) Use '**or**' to give an **alternative**.

> We could go shopping tomorrow, **or** we could go bowling.

Practice Questions

1) Choose 'and', 'or', 'so', 'because' or 'but' to complete these sentences.

   a) I will either buy a T-shirt .... some trousers from the shop.

   b) I can't come to the meeting today .... I have a dental appointment.

   c) I'm going to cut the cake into slices .... that everyone gets some.

   d) They would have come over, ... they already had tickets for a play.

   e) He couldn't decide whether to wait for her .... leave without her.

   f) She's always loved baking cakes .... knitting.

   g) You can't put that glass there .... it will fall off and break.

   h) Ted wanted to win the singing competition, ... he practiced every night.

2) Your friend has asked you to go to a restaurant for dinner on 2nd February and then go to a concert afterwards. He has suggested you go for dinner at 7 pm so that you can get to the concert for 10 pm (when it starts). You would like to go for dinner, although you have to pick your brother up from work at 10:30 pm.

   Write a short reply to your friend, explaining why you can only go for dinner. Use the joining words 'so', 'if', 'because', 'until', and 'but'. You don't need to worry about layout.

   ....

   ....

   ....

   ....

   ....

   ....

   ....

   ....

Using Joining Words to Link Ideas

Joining words can help structure your writing

Use **joining words** to link your **sentences** together to make **paragraphs**.

> I agree that traffic is a problem on our roads, but drivers need to use their cars to get to work. Therefore, I am against the ban on cars.

'But' and 'therefore' make this paragraph flow better.

Use joining words to put your points in order

1) Use '**firstly**' to introduce your **most important point**.

> Firstly, I think the most important issue is obesity...

'Firstly', 'secondly' and 'finally' are usually only used in formal texts.

2) Use '**secondly**' to make your **next point**.

> Secondly, another issue is P.E. in schools...

You could use 'in addition' or 'furthermore' instead of 'secondly'.

3) Use '**finally**' to round off your argument.

> Finally, I want you to make school meals healthier...

You could use 'in conclusion' or 'therefore' instead of 'finally'.

Use 'however' and 'therefore' to develop your writing

1) Use '**therefore**' to explain a result.

2) '**However**' can be used to disagree with something that has just been said.

> Litter is a big problem. Therefore, I think more needs to be done about it. However, graffiti is an even bigger issue.

You could also use 'consequently' or 'as a result'.

You could also use 'although' or 'nevertheless'.

Using Joining Words to Link Ideas

Use 'for example' to add an example

Use **'for example'** to back up your point.

> Owning a pet can be expensive — for example, there can be quite a lot of costly vet's bills.

You could also use 'for instance'.

Practice Questions

1) Choose 'therefore', 'for example' or 'however' to complete these sentences.

   a) I broke my leg. .... , I couldn't play football.

   b) It was very rainy. .... , it was still quite warm.

   c) I'm a really bad cook. .... , I once set the oven on fire.

   d) The tyres need changing. .... , the lorry isn't safe to drive.

   e) I want to go somewhere warm on holiday this year. .... , Greece or Spain.

   f) He was angry when he got to work. .... , he cheered up later in the day.

2) Use 'firstly', 'secondly', 'therefore', 'for example' and 'however' to complete this text.

   .... , the main argument for banning mobile phones is that they can be harmful and cause all sorts of problems. .... , if they are used while driving, they can lead to road traffic accidents.

   .... , mobile phones are bad for your health. Some reports suggest that texting could cause arthritis.

   .... , mobile phones have become an important part of everyday life, and they help people stay in touch with their friends and family. .... , I think we should think carefully about how much we use mobile phones, and try to avoid using them where possible.

Using Different Verb Tenses

A verb is a doing or being word

Verbs tell you what something **does** or **is**.

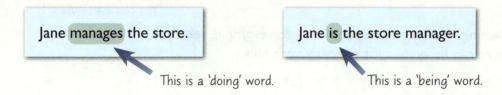

Jane manages the store.

This is a 'doing' word.

Jane is the store manager.

This is a 'being' word.

Use the present tense to say what is happening now

Most verbs in the **present tense** follow the same **verb pattern**:

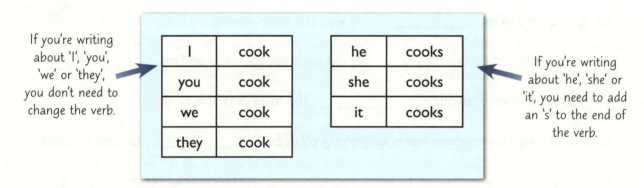

If you're writing about 'I', 'you', 'we' or 'they', you don't need to change the verb.

I	cook
you	cook
we	cook
they	cook

he	cooks
she	cooks
it	cooks

If you're writing about 'he', 'she' or 'it', you need to add an 's' to the end of the verb.

How you change the verb depends on who is doing it

Use the **verb pattern** to work out the correct ending.

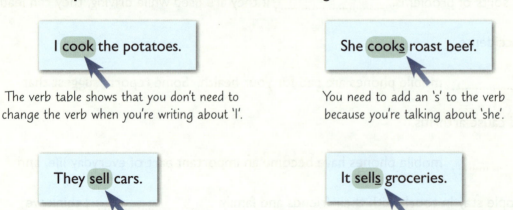

I cook the potatoes.

The verb table shows that you don't need to change the verb when you're writing about 'I'.

She cooks roast beef.

You need to add an 's' to the verb because you're talking about 'she'.

They sell cars.

You don't need to change the verb when you're writing about 'they'.

It sells groceries.

You need to add an 's' to the verb because you're talking about 'it'.

Using Different Verb Tenses

Use the past tense to say what has already happened

1) Most verbs need '**ed**' at the end to make them into the past tense.

ask ➝ I asked   talk ➝ they talked

2) If the verb already ends in '**e**', just add a '**d**' to the end.

bake ➝ she baked   chase ➝ he chased

Not all past tense verbs add 'ed'

1) Some common verbs **act differently**:

Use 'was' for 'I', 'he', 'she' and 'it'.
Use 'were' for 'you', 'we' and 'they'.

Verb	Past Tense
to do	did
to have	had
to see	saw
to get	got
to take	took

Verb	Past Tense
to be	was / were
to go	went
to make	made
to come	came
to think	thought

These are just a few examples. There are other verbs that act differently too.

2) Some verbs **don't change** at all in the past tense:

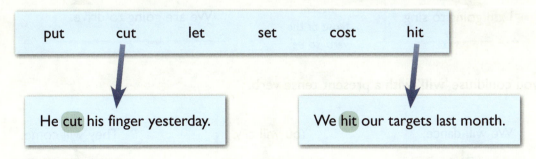

put   cut   let   set   cost   hit

He cut his finger yesterday.   We hit our targets last month.

Section Three — Using Grammar

Using Different Verb Tenses

Use 'have' to talk about recent actions

1) To talk about recent actions, you need **two parts**.

   • The first part is '**has**' or '**have**'.

   • For most verbs, the second part is the **same** as the normal past tense.

2) Use '**have**' with 'I', 'you', 'we' and 'they'. Use '**has**' with 'he', 'she' and 'it'.

This is the past tense of 'walk'.

This uses 'have' to talk about the recent past.

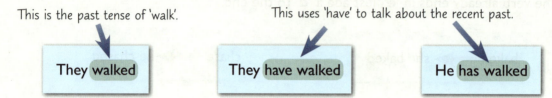

They walked   They have walked   He has walked

3) For some verbs, the second part is **different** to the normal past tense:

Verb	with 'have'	Verb	with 'have'
to do	has / have done	to go	has / have gone
to be	has / have been	to write	has / have written
to see	has / have seen	to take	has / have taken

They took   They have taken   She has taken

There are two ways to talk about the future

1) Talk about future actions by using '**am**', '**is**' or '**are**' and the verb '**going**'.

I am going to sing.

This is the present tense of the verb 'to be'.

We are going to drive.

Use a verb with 'to' in front of it after 'going'.

2) Or you could use '**will**' with a present tense verb.

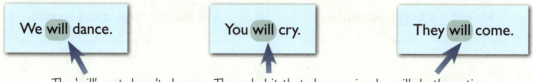

We will dance.   You will cry.   They will come.

The 'will' part doesn't change. The only bit that changes is who will do the action.

Using Different Verb Tenses

Stay in the same tense in your writing

1) All the verbs in your writing need to be **consistent** with each other.

2) This means verbs that are in the **same sentence** usually need to be in the **same tense**.

> I work in London where it is very busy and noisy.

'Work' and 'is' are both in the present tense — they agree with each other.

> When they went to Paris they visited the Eiffel Tower and speak French.

'Went' and 'visited' are both in the past tense — they agree with each other.

'Speak' is in the present tense, so the sentence doesn't make sense — the verb should be 'spoke'.

Practice Questions

1) Rewrite each sentence in the past tense. Use the normal past tense (not with 'have').

a) She has pasta for dinner.

....

b) I see a field of sheep on the way to work.

....

c) We go to the festival.

....

2) Rewrite these sentences to be about the future. Use 'will' in your answers.

a) I made an apple crumble.

....

b) He came to football practice.

....

c) They were angry.

....

Using Modal Verbs

Modal verbs change the meaning of a sentence

1) Modal verbs can show how **likely** something is, your **ability** to do something, or whether you **need** to do something.

2) They come **before** the **main verb** and **change the meaning** of the sentence.

We could buy another photocopier. ← The word 'could' shows the possibility of buying another photocopier.

3) Here are the **main ones**:

can	could	may	might	shall	should	will	would	must

They can show how possible or desirable something is

1) Modal verbs can be used to show how **possible** something is:

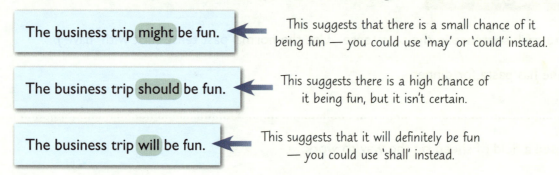

The business trip might be fun. ← This suggests that there is a small chance of it being fun — you could use 'may' or 'could' instead.

The business trip should be fun. ← This suggests there is a high chance of it being fun, but it isn't certain.

The business trip will be fun. ← This suggests that it will definitely be fun — you could use 'shall' instead.

2) They can also show how much someone **wants** something:

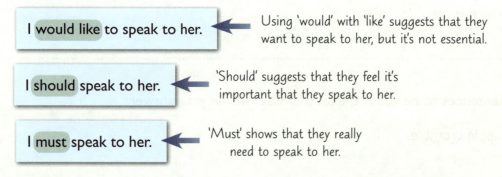

I would like to speak to her. ← Using 'would' with 'like' suggests that they want to speak to her, but it's not essential.

I should speak to her. ← 'Should' suggests that they feel it's important that they speak to her.

I must speak to her. ← 'Must' shows that they really need to speak to her.

You can make most of these verbs into negatives

1) Here are the **main ones**:

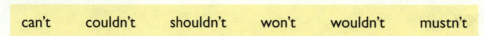

can't	couldn't	shouldn't	won't	wouldn't	mustn't

2) These negative verbs are the **informal** versions.

3) **Formal** versions just use 'not', e.g. '**might not**' or '**shall not**'.

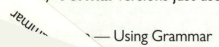

— Using Grammar

Practice Questions

1) Underline the modal verb in each sentence.

   a) Damien might get an invite to the conference if he's lucky.

   b) I can play the piano, but I play the violin better.

   c) Don't worry, I shall make sure I tell them tomorrow.

   d) It should not be too cold, but take your coat just in case.

2) Circle the option that best fits in each sentence.

   a) I need some more paper, so I **can / will** go to the shops tomorrow.

   b) She **would / will** go to the party if she was allowed.

   c) I **might / must** remember to turn off the oven or the food will burn.

   d) He was late and so **couldn't / mustn't** make the meeting.

3) Use 'might', 'must', 'could' or 'should' to complete these sentences. Use each one once.

   a) You .... do a criminal record check before you can apply.

   b) It's likely to rain at the construction site, so you .... bring a coat.

   c) Shelley .... fix the car herself, but she decided to take it to the garage.

   d) I .... start an apprenticeship, but I haven't decided yet.

4) Write a sentence of your own for each of the verbs below.

   a) **can** ....

   ....

   b) **won't** ....

   ....

   c) **would** ....

   ....

   d) **mustn't** ....

   ....

Common Mistakes With Verbs

A verb must agree with the person doing the action

1) Check **who** is doing the action to work out if the **verb** should **change**.

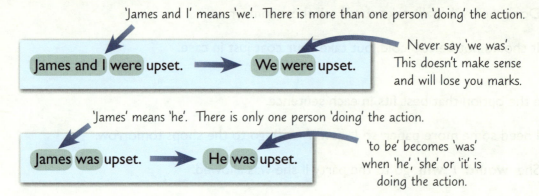

'James and I' means 'we'. There is more than one person 'doing' the action.

James and I were upset. ➡ We were upset.

Never say 'we was'. This doesn't make sense and will lose you marks.

'James' means 'he'. There is only one person 'doing' the action.

James was upset. ➡ He was upset.

'to be' becomes 'was' when 'he', 'she' or 'it' is doing the action.

2) To say 'there **is**' or 'there **are**', use the right '**being**' word to match the person.

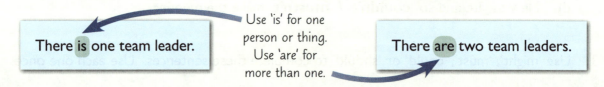

There is one team leader.

Use 'is' for one person or thing. Use 'are' for more than one.

There are two team leaders.

'Been' and 'done' always go with 'have' or 'has'

Always use '**have**' or '**has**' when you write 'been' or 'done'.

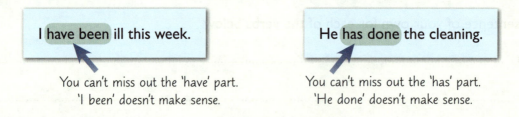

I have been ill this week.

You can't miss out the 'have' part. 'I been' doesn't make sense.

He has done the cleaning.

You can't miss out the 'has' part. 'He done' doesn't make sense.

Don't confuse 'could've' with 'could of'

1) Always write '**could have**'. Never write 'could of' because it doesn't mean anything.

2) It's the same for '**might have**' and '**should have**'.

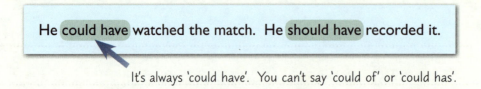

He could have watched the match. He should have recorded it.

It's always 'could have'. You can't say 'could of' or 'could has'.

Common Mistakes With Verbs

'Don't' means 'do not' and 'doesn't' means 'does not'

1) Use '**don't**' with 'I', 'you', 'we' and 'they'.

2) Use '**doesn't**' with 'he', 'she' and 'it'.

I don't want to leave.

This is short for 'I do not'.

He doesn't drink coffee.

This is short for 'He does not'.

Practice Questions

1) A verb in each of these sentences is wrong. Rewrite the sentence without any mistakes.

a) There are one cat.

....

b) Priya don't work on Mondays.

....

c) We was on the train to London.

....

d) The men have being on holiday.

....

2) Rewrite each sentence so that it makes sense.

a) She might of broken her leg.

....

b) They could of cleaned the house.

....

c) I should of gone with him to the bank.

....

Punctuating Sentences

Every sentence should start with a capital letter

1) **Every sentence** should begin with a **capital letter**.

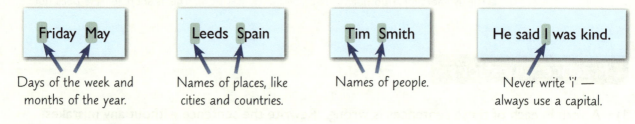

| The supermarket is always open. | | Libraries are quiet places. |

2) Some words begin with a **capital letter** even in the **middle** of a sentence.

| Friday May | Leeds Spain | Tim Smith | He said I was kind. |

Days of the week and
months of the year.

Names of places, like
cities and countries.

Names of people.

Never write 'i' —
always use a capital.

Most sentences end with a full stop

1) Use a **full stop** to show that your sentence has **finished**.

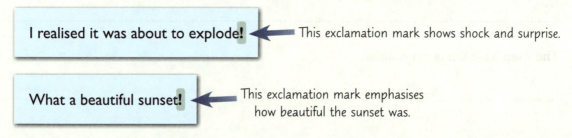

The fridge was shaking. He looked behind it.

2) Use an **exclamation mark** if you're saying something really **amazing**.

I realised it was about to explode! ← This exclamation mark shows shock and surprise.

What a beautiful sunset! ← This exclamation mark emphasises
how beautiful the sunset was.

3) Try not to use **too many** exclamation marks. If you're not sure, use a **full stop instead**.

4) You should also avoid using exclamation marks in **formal** writing.

Questions end with question marks

1) A question should **start** with a **capital letter**...

2) ...but it should end with a **question mark** instead of a full stop.

Is he angry? ← Use a question mark here.
You don't need a full stop as well.

Practice Questions

1) Use capital letters and full stops to write these sentences correctly.
   You might need to write two sentences instead of one.

   a) the trees in scotland were about 50 ft high

   ....

   b) on monday she slipped and fell over crossing the river

   ....

   c) hiking isn't much fun with the wrong shoes

   ....

   d) I don't know where he is he might have gone shopping in manchester

   ....

   ....

   e) polar bears are known to be violent i hope we don't see one

   ....

   ....

   f) she advertised his sofa in the newspaper she sold it for £100

   ....

   ....

2) Use a full stop, an exclamation mark or a question mark to end each sentence correctly.

   a) Why are there so many horror films out at the moment......

   b) It turned out that his own brother was the villain...... That surprised everyone......

   c) We went to see the football last night...... The second half was amazing......

   d) That's awful...... We should do something about it......

   e) How can you like that band...... I don't think they're any good......

   f) They've sold more records this year than last year...... How have they done that......

Using Commas

Commas separate things in a list

1) **Commas** can **break up lists** of **three** or **more** things.

2) Put a **comma** after **each thing** in the list.

3) Between the **last two things** you **don't** need a **comma**. Use **'and'** or **'or'** instead.

Today I ate a banana, a pear, some chocolate and a sandwich.

You don't need a comma here — use 'and' instead.

Commas split up the information so it's easier to read.

Commas can join two points

There's more about joining words on p.82-85.

1) **Two sentences** can be **joined** using a **joining word** and a **comma**.

2) **Joining words** are words like **'and'**, **'but'** and **'so'**.

3) The comma is added **before** the joining word to show where the new sentence **begins**.

I was thirsty today, so I drank lots of water.

Don't use too many commas. Shorter sentences separated with full stops are easier to understand.

The comma and 'so' join the two sentences together.

Commas can separate extra information

1) **Extra information** in a sentence can be **separated** using **commas**.

2) Extra information adds **detail**, but you **don't need it** for the sentence to **make sense**.

The restaurant, which was open all night, had great-value meals.

The bit in between the commas is extra information.

3) To check if you've used these commas correctly, **remove** the words **inside** the **commas**.

The restaurant had great-value meals.

If the sentence still makes sense, then you're using them correctly.

Using Commas

Extra information can begin or end a sentence

1) Sometimes the extra information can come at the **start** of a sentence.

2) In this case, you only need to use **one** comma rather than **two**.

> When he had chosen a car, Chris signed the contract.

The first bit of the sentence is extra information — it's separated from the second part with a comma.

3) The extra information could also come at the **end** of the sentence.

4) In this case, you **don't** need to use a comma to separate the two parts of the sentence.

> Chris signed the contract when he had chosen a car.

When the extra information comes **after** the main information, it doesn't need a comma.

Practice Questions

1) Correct these sentences by putting commas in the right places.

   a) You need to add cinnamon nutmeg and vanilla to the cake mix.

   b) The cat which looked like a stray was very friendly.

   c) James injured his shoulder so he couldn't go bowling.

   d) The bookshop sells biographies thrillers and romances.

   e) Although the cinema was full it was completely silent.

   f) Would you like chocolate chip vanilla or strawberry ice cream?

   g) They were going to go to the concert but they missed the bus.

   h) Alex Johns who was my best man never made it to the wedding.

   i) Our team reached the finals so we went out to celebrate.

   j) I want chopped onions lettuce peppers and tomatoes in my sandwich.

   k) Jim and Maher were going to London but they changed their minds.

   l) The flat-pack table which had instructions with it was easy to build.

   m) The café which sold lots of different types of tea was very popular.

Using Apostrophes

Apostrophes show that letters are missing

1) An **apostrophe** looks like this — ,

2) Apostrophes show where letters have been **removed**.

The apostrophe shows that the 'a' of 'are' has been removed.

The apostrophe shows that the 'w' and 'i' of 'will' have been removed.

Apostrophes show something belongs to someone

1) Use an **apostrophe** and an **'s'** to show that someone **owns** something.

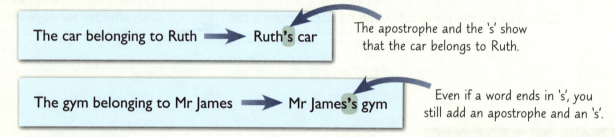

The apostrophe and the 's' show that the car belongs to Ruth.

Even if a word ends in 's', you still add an apostrophe and an 's'.

2) If a plural ends in **'s'**, you just need to add an **apostrophe** to the end of the word.

The buses' schedules are new.

3) If a plural **doesn't** end in **'s'**, you should add an **apostrophe** and **'s'**.

The men's toilets are locked.

'it's' and 'its' mean different things

1) **'It's'** with an apostrophe means 'it is' or 'it has'.

2) The **apostrophe** shows that there are **letters missing**.

It is time for lunch. → It's time for lunch.

The apostrophe shows that the 'i' is missing from 'is'.

3) **'Its'** without an apostrophe means 'belonging to it'.

The dog loved its new toy.

This shows that the toy belongs to the dog.

The shop was changing its name.

This shows that the name belongs to the shop.

Using Apostrophes

Don't use apostrophes for plurals

Never use an apostrophe to show that there's **more than one** of something.   This is wrong.

| two phones   NOT   two phone's |

| some ducks   NOT   some duck's |

Practice Questions

1) Shorten these phrases by putting apostrophes in the correct places.

   a) have not ....   d) could not ....

   b) you will ....   e) you are ....

   c) I would ....   f) did not ....

2) Rewrite these sentences using apostrophes to show who owns what.

   a) the car park belonging to the office

   ....

   b) the sweets belonging to the child

   ....

   c) the fingerprints belonging to the burglar

   ....

   d) the uniform belonging to the nurse

   ....

3) Circle the correct word to use in each sentence.

   a) **It's / Its** not surprising that **it's / its** fallen over.

   b) The team won **it's / its** final match. **It's / Its** unbelievable!

   c) **It's / Its** so nice to see your cat and **it's / its** kittens.

Inverted Commas and Quotation Marks

Inverted commas and quotation marks come in pairs

1) **Inverted commas** look a bit like apostrophes ❝❞ . They always come in **pairs**.

2) One goes at the **beginning** of a word or phrase, the other goes at the **end**.

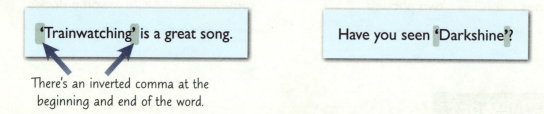

| 'Trainwatching' is a great song. | Have you seen 'Darkshine'? |

There's an inverted comma at the beginning and end of the word.

3) **Quotation marks** look like **two** apostrophes ❝❞ .

| "I'll come to yours at 7 pm." | "Stop right there," she said. |

Like inverted commas, quotation marks always come in twos.

Inverted commas are used for titles

Titles of things, for example books or films, usually go inside **inverted commas**.

| He bought a copy of 'On the River'. | I watched 'Green's Anatomy' last night. |

Quotation marks are used to quote

Quotation marks go around the **actual words** that **someone says**.

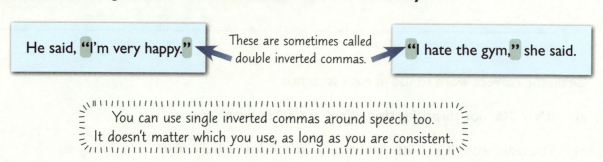

| He said, "I'm very happy." | "I hate the gym," she said. |

These are sometimes called double inverted commas.

You can use single inverted commas around speech too.
It doesn't matter which you use, as long as you are consistent.

Inverted Commas and Quotation Marks

Quoted speech needs to be punctuated correctly

1) Always start the **first word of speech** with a **capital letter**, even if it's in the middle of a sentence.

2) If your **sentence ends** when the **speech ends**, put a **full stop** before the last quotation mark.

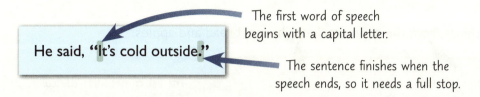

The first word of speech begins with a capital letter.

He said, "It's cold outside."

The sentence finishes when the speech ends, so it needs a full stop.

3) If the **sentence continues** after the speech, put a **comma** before the last quotation mark.

4) You can also end speech with an **exclamation mark** or a **question mark**.

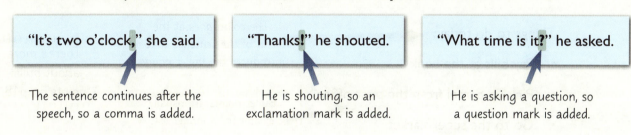

"It's two o'clock," she said.

The sentence continues after the speech, so a comma is added.

"Thanks!" he shouted.

He is shouting, so an exclamation mark is added.

"What time is it?" he asked.

He is asking a question, so a question mark is added.

Practice Questions

1) Correct these sentences by putting inverted commas in the right places.

a) Have you read his new book, Glimpsing Heaven ?

b) It's the first time I've ever seen The Woman in Blue .

c) The Sparkshire Herald is full of interesting articles .

2) Rewrite these sentences using punctuation in the correct places.

a) Happy Birthday we all shouted together

....

....

b) The supporters shouted come on Hadych you can do it

....

....

Using Colons

Colons are used for introducing lists

1) **Colons** looked like two stacked full stops $\vdots$.

2) They are used to introduce **extra information**, so are often used in **lists**.

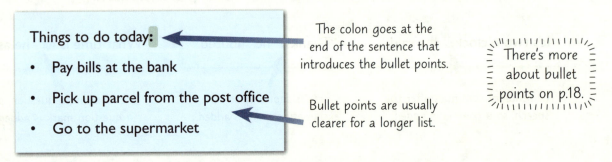

I need three things from the supermarket: cheese, bread and apples.

This is the main sentence.
It normally makes sense by itself.

The colon
introduces the list.

The list comes after the colon.

3) You can also use a colon to introduce a list of **bullet points.**

Things to do today:

* Pay bills at the bank

* Pick up parcel from the post office

* Go to the supermarket

The colon goes at the
end of the sentence that
introduces the bullet points.

Bullet points are usually
clearer for a longer list.

There's more
about bullet
points on p.18.

Colons can also introduce explanations

1) **Colons** can be used to join two sentences together.

2) Use a colon when the **second sentence** explains something in the **first**.

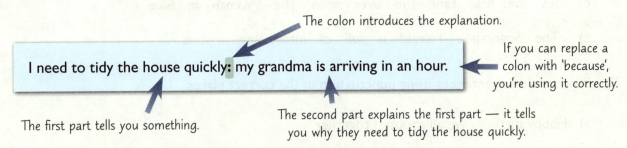

The colon introduces the explanation.

I need to tidy the house quickly: my grandma is arriving in an hour.

If you can replace a
colon with 'because',
you're using it correctly.

The first part tells you something.

The second part explains the first part — it tells
you why they need to tidy the house quickly.

Remember the golden rule when using colons

To help you remember when you can use a colon, follow this **golden rule**:

first point: more specific point

This is always related to the first point.
It gives more information or an explanation.

Practice Questions

1) Rewrite the following sentence as a list of bullets.

> I need to do three things before the interview: iron my shirt, print my CV and make a packed lunch.

....

- *iron my shirt*
- *Print my CV*
- *Make a packed lunch*

2) Rewrite each of these lists as a full sentence that uses a colon.

a)

Holiday shopping list:
• Sun cream
• Swimwear
• A beach towel

....

....

....

b)

Facilities at the sports centre:
• A swimming pool
• A climbing wall
• A gymnasium

....

....

....

3) Correct these sentences by putting colons in the right places.

a) Margaret has three children Robin, Joseph and Emma.

b) Last year I visited three countries Portugal, Croatia and Estonia.

c) Tim is holding a bake sale he's raising money for charity.

d) The recipe only needed two more ingredients parsnips and carrots.

e) Amy isn't coming to the party she is going on holiday.

f) Petra always takes the stairs she is terrified of lifts.

g) The dog barked loudly at the tree it had seen a cat.

h) The greenhouse is full of fruit strawberries, raspberries and tomatoes.

i) Erik is free on Tuesday afternoon his French lessons have finished.

Spelling Tricks

The 'i' before 'e' rule

1) 'i' and 'e' often appear **next to each other** in a word.

2) This means it can be **tricky** to **remember** which comes **first**.

3) Use the **'i' before 'e' rule** to help:

'i' before 'e' except after 'c', but only when it rhymes with 'bee'.

The 'ie' sound rhymes with 'bee', so 'i' goes before 'e'.

The 'ie' sound rhymes with 'bee', but there's a 'c', so the 'e' goes before 'i'.

The 'ie' sound doesn't rhyme with 'bee', so 'e' goes before 'i'.

The 'ie' sound comes after 'c', but it doesn't rhyme with 'bee', so 'i' goes before 'e'.

A few words don't follow the rule

Watch out for these **tricky examples**.

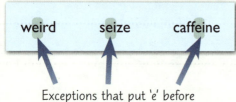
Exceptions that put 'e' before 'i' that rhyme with bee.

The 'i' goes before the 'e', even though it comes after 'c' and rhymes with 'bee'.

Use memorable phrases to help you spell tricky words

Make up **sentences** or **phrases** to remind you how words are spelt.

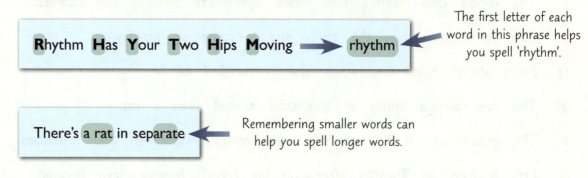
The first letter of each word in this phrase helps you spell 'rhythm'.

Remembering smaller words can help you spell longer words.

Practice Questions

1) Rewrite each word so that it is spelt correctly. Some words may already be correct.

   a) recieve ....   d) fierce ....

   b) science ....   e) freind ....

   c) acheive ....   f) wierd ....

2) Think of four words that you find tricky to spell. Look up the spelling of each word in a dictionary and write it in the box. Think of a phrase that will help you remember how to spell it.

   [box]

   ....

   ....

   [box]

   ....

   ....

   [box]

   ....

   ....

   [box]

   ....

   ....

Making Plurals

Plural means 'more than one'

1) To make most words **plural**, you add an **'s'** on the **end**.

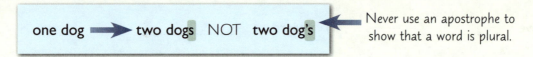

one dog ➡ two dogs   NOT   two dog's

Never use an apostrophe to show that a word is plural.

2) If a word **ends** with **'ch'**, **'x'**, **'s'**, **'sh'** or **'z'**, put **'es'** on the **end** to make it plural.

| two torches | some foxes | many glasses | three dishes | the waltzes |

Words ending with 'y' have different rules

1) Some words end with a **vowel** ('a', 'e', 'i', 'o' or 'u') and then a **'y'** (for example b**oy**).

2) To make these words **plural**, put an **'s'** on the end. For example, 'tray' becomes 'tray**s**'.

3) Some words end with a **consonant** (any letter that isn't a **vowel**) and then a **'y'**.

4) To make them **plural**, change the **'y'** to an **'i'** and then add **'es'** on the **end**.

cry ➡ cries   county ➡ counties

't' is a consonant, so the ending changes.

Words ending with 'f' or 'fe' need a 'v'

1) To make words ending with **'f' plural**, change the **'f'** to a **'v'** and add **'es'**.

one shelf ➡ two shelves   a thief ➡ three thieves

2) To make words ending with **'fe' plural**, change the **'f'** to a **'v'** and add **'s'**.

one wife ➡ two wives   a knife ➡ three knives

Making Plurals

Some words don't follow a pattern

1) To make some words **plural**, you have to change the **spelling** of the word.

2) Some words **don't change at all**.

You would always say 'two sheep', never 'two sheeps'.

Practice Questions

1) Write the plural of each word.

a) cinema ....

e) baby ....

b) Friday ....

f) half ....

c) brush ....

g) reindeer ....

d) journey ....

h) monkey ....

2) Rewrite each of these sentences with the correct plurals.

a) The boyes ate all the peachs.

....

b) The puppys played in the leafs.

....

c) The branchs were burnt to ashs.

....

d) The spys carried gadgets that looked like scarfs.

....

Adding Prefixes and Suffixes

Prefixes and suffixes are used to make new words

1) **Prefixes** are **letters** that are added to the **start** of words.

2) When you add a **prefix**, it **changes** the **meaning** of the word.

3) **Suffixes** are letters that are added to the **end** of words.

4) When you add a **suffix**, it also **changes** the **meaning** of the word.

 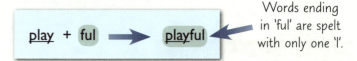

Words ending in 'ful' are spelt with only one 'l'.

Adding a prefix doesn't change the spelling

If you add a **prefix** to a word, the **spelling** of the **word stays the same**.

The spelling of the prefix and the word don't change.

Adding a suffix might change the spelling

1) If you add a **suffix** to a word, sometimes the spelling **changes**.

2) If a word ends in an 'e' and the **first letter** of the suffix is a **vowel**, you **drop** the 'e'.

3) If a word ends with a **consonant** and then a 'y', change the 'y' to an 'i'.

When you add a suffix, ignore the 'i' before 'e' rule.

Adding Prefixes and Suffixes

The C-V-C rule tells you when to double letters

1) If you're adding a **suffix** that begins with a **vowel**, you can use the **C-V-C rule**.

2) For most words, if the last three letters go **consonant - vowel - consonant (C-V-C)**...

All these words end with C-V-C.

3) ...you **double** the **last letter** when you add the **suffix**.

'ing' starts with a vowel, so double the 't'.

4) If the **first letter** of the **suffix** is a **consonant**, you **don't** double the last letter.

'ness' starts with a consonant, so don't double the 'd'.

Practice Questions

1) Rewrite these words so they are spelt correctly. Some words may already be correct.

a) stopper   ....

b) hopefull   ....

c) lovely   ....

d) repplay   ....

e) beautyful   ....

f) misslead   ....

2) Rewrite each of these sentences and correct the mistakes.

a) He tried to help the joger.

....

b) She was fameous for her kinddness.

....

c) I am puting this sillyness behind me.

....

Section Five — Using Correct Spelling

Common Spelling Mistakes

Words with double letters can be hard to spell

1) It's tricky to spell words with **double letters** because you **can't hear them** when they're said.

2) **Learn** how to spell these **common** words with **double letters**.

| different | tomorrow | professional | address |

| necessary | immediate | occasionally | success |

Some words have more than one double letter.

Silent letters and unclear sounds can be tricky

1) Sometimes you **can't hear** a certain **letter** when you say a word.

2) These are known as **silent letters**.

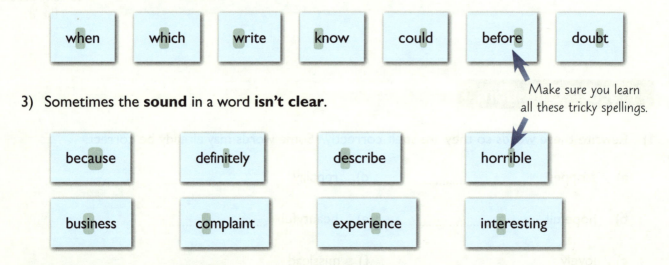

| when | which | write | know | could | before | doubt |

3) Sometimes the **sound** in a word **isn't clear**.

Make sure you learn all these tricky spellings.

| because | definitely | describe | horrible |

| business | complaint | experience | interesting |

Make sure you're using the right word

1) '**A lot**' means '**many**' — always write it as **two separate** words. '**Alot**' is **not** a real word.

2) '**Thank you**' is always written as **two words**.

3) '**As well**' is always written as two separate words. '**Aswell**' is **not** a real word.

4) '**Maybe**' means '**perhaps**'. '**May be**' means '**might be**'.

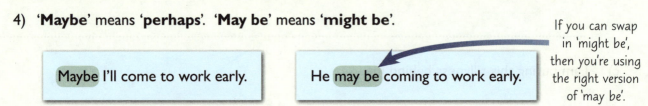

Maybe I'll come to work early.

He may be coming to work early.

If you can swap in 'might be', then you're using the right version of 'may be'.

Practice Questions

1) Each of these sentences has two mistakes. Correct the mistakes and rewrite the sentence.

a) He will rite to you tommorow.

....

b) Wich hotel have you stayed at befor?

....

c) You can wear this on many diferent ocasions.

....

d) Do you know wen you cud come in?

....

e) I've had alot of problems with my laptop aswell.

....

f) Do you no the adress of that company?

....

g) My experiance has been horibble.

....

h) We hired you becos you're proffesional.

....

i) A sucesful company doesn't receive cumplaints.

....

j) I will definately use your busness again.

....

k) It maybe a leak, but I dout it.

....

l) Is it neccesary to do this imediately?

....

Spelling Specialist Words

Some words are used to talk about certain topics

1) **Specialist** words are used when you're talking about **particular topics**.

2) For example, the words '**runway**' and '**departures**' are specialist words for the topic of **airports**.

3) Some specialist words have a **specific meaning** when they're used in certain **contexts**.

4) For example, 'runway' has a different meaning when linked with **airports** than with **fashion**.

Some specialist words can be shortened

1) Many specialist words are often **shortened**.

2) Make sure you can spell the **full word** so you can use it in **formal writing**.

exam ➔ examination   advert ➔ advertisement

Specialist words are sometimes tricky to spell

1) Specialist words can be **hard to spell**.

2) Some have **lots of letters**, like '**administration**' or '**productivity**'.

3) Some have **double letters**.

Baccalaureate   accessibility   committee

Some have more than one double letter.

4) Some have **silent letters** or **unclear sounds**.

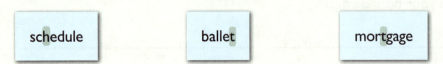

schedule   ballet   mortgage

5) Some **don't** follow the **rules**.

protein   Some don't follow the 'i' before 'e' rule.

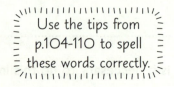

Use the tips from p.104-110 to spell these words correctly.

Practice Questions

1) Rewrite the following sentences with the full version of the word in bold.

   a) I've got so much **vocab** to learn for my French exam.

   ....

   b) The sales **rep** from the travel agency is very friendly.

   ....

   c) Did you see Keeley's **photos** from her summer holiday?

   ....

   d) He had to **prep** the food for his mother's party.

   ....

2) Each of these sentences has a mistake. Correct the mistake and rewrite the sentence.

   a) The train is always so busy on my morning comute.

   ....

   b) The deadline for these asignments is in two weeks.

   ....

   c) Aisha and Charlotte could finally get a morgage.

   ....

   d) You will be marked on how well you colaborate.

   ....

   e) She's been awarded a scolarship by her university.

   ....

   f) We need to consider the profitibility of this project.

   ....

   g) The flat comes part-fernished and is available now.

   ....

Commonly Confused Words

'Their', 'they're' and 'there' are all different

1) **'Their'** means 'belonging to them'.

> Their flat has two bedrooms.

> He took their warning seriously.

2) **'They're'** means 'they are'.

> They're living in a two-bed flat.

> They're giving him a warning.

If you can replace 'they're' with 'they are', and the sentence makes sense, then it's right.

3) **'There'** can be used to talk about a **location**...

> The flat is over there.

> They are there now.

4) ...or to **introduce a sentence**.

> There are two choices.

> There is no reason to give him a warning.

Learn how to use 'to' and 'too'

1) **'To'** can mean 'towards' or it can be part of a **verb**.

> He's going to Spain.

When 'to' means 'towards', it's followed by a place or an event.

> Tell him to meet me at 7 pm.

'To' is often followed by a verb.

2) **'Too'** can mean 'too much' or it can mean 'also'.

> This soup is too hot.

When 'too' means 'too much', it often has a describing word after it.

> She's going to the gig too.

When 'too' means 'also', it usually comes at the end of a sentence.

Commonly Confused Words

'You're' and 'your' mean different things

1) **'You're'** means 'you are'.

   If you can replace 'you're' with 'you are' and the sentence makes sense, then it's the right word.

   You're working twice this week.

2) **'Your'** means 'belonging to you'.

   Keep your uniform in your locker.

   The uniform belongs to you.

Don't confuse 'off' and 'of'

1) **'Off'** can mean 'not on'. **'Off'** can also mean 'away (from)'.

   Turn the lights off.

   I took Monday off work.

2) **'Of'** is a **linking word**. It **joins parts** of a sentence **together**.

   My wardrobe is full of clothes I don't wear.

'Are' and 'our' sound alike

1) **'Are'** is a **verb** (doing word).

   We are paid every Friday.

   Are we going out tonight?

   This is asking whether something might happen.

2) **'Our'** means 'belonging to us'.

   It's our favourite song.

   Our house is near the church.

   This shows who owns something.

Commonly Confused Words

'Been' and 'being' can sound the same

1) **'Been'** is used after the words **'have'**, **'has'** or **'had'**.

> I have been there before.

> Dad has been too.

> My aunt had been before us both.

2) **'Being'** is used after **'am'**, **'are'**, **'were'** or **'was'**.

> I am being helpful.

> They are being helped.

> We were being kind.

> Lucy was being thoughtful.

'Bought' and 'brought' mean different things

'Brought' is the past tense of **'bring'**. **'Bought'** is the past tense of **'buy'**.

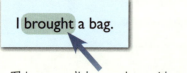

> I brought a bag.

> I bought a bag.

This means 'I have a bag with me'.

This means 'I purchased a bag'.

'Teach' and 'learn' are opposites

1) You **teach** information **to** someone else.

2) You **learn** information **from** someone else.

> I teach Italian to my mother.

> My mother learns Italian from me.

Practice Questions

1) Circle the correct word to use in each sentence.

   a) **Are / Our** there **too / to** many people on board?

   b) I hope **you're / your** joking when you say **you're / your** going to buy a snake.

   c) **Their / They're** going to go **to / too** bed.

   d) He was **being / been** careless with **you're / your** car.

   e) Can you **learn / teach** me how to use **our / are** dishwasher?

2) Each of these sentences has two mistakes. Correct the mistakes and rewrite the sentence.

   a) They bought they're dog into work.

   ....

   b) There going to far this time.

   ....

   c) She wants to learn her son how too be polite.

   ....

   d) I think your tired off long hours.

   ....

   e) I want too teach cooking from an expert.

   ....

   f) Toby's being to the gym. Have you been going their too?

   ....

   g) I brought it from that new shop over their.

   ....

   h) Are you're children been naughty?

   ....

   i) Their is the cake I bought into work.

   ....

Writing Test Advice

You will have two tasks to do in the writing test

1) In the writing test, you will have **one hour** and **twenty minutes** to do **two** tasks.

2) Use the number of **marks** available for each question to help you split up your **time**. If both questions are worth the same amount of marks, spend an **equal** amount of time on them.

3) Look for any suggested **word counts** or for a suggested **number of paragraphs** you should write.

Planning is important in the writing test

1) Making a **plan** will help you get your ideas in the **right order**.

2) If you're given **bullet points**, make sure you use them in your plan.

> If you're doing your test onscreen, you can still use a pen and paper to write down rough work.

EXAMPLE:

A half-marathon is taking place in Manchester to raise money for a children's charity.

- Are sponsored events a good way to raise money?

- Apart from raising money, how else do charities benefit from large-scale fundraising events?

- Should more people take part in sponsored events?

Write an email to persuade your co-workers to take part in the half-marathon.

> It might be helpful to write about the bullet points in the order they are given.

3) You will get marks if your answer has a **clear beginning**, **middle** and **end**.

4) **Don't** spend **too long** on your plan — leave enough time to write your **full answer**.

5) Try to leave some time at the end of the test to **check** your work and **correct any mistakes**.

Write clearly and correctly in the writing test

1) Use **full sentences** and **paragraphs** to make your writing clear.

2) **Spelling**, **punctuation** and **grammar** are worth **44%** of the marks, so **check** for mistakes.

3) Your **style** and **content** are **important**:

- **Don't** use words like 'coz' or 'tho', even if you're writing to a friend.

- Always be **polite**. Even if you are writing to complain, **don't be rude**.

- If you **make up any details**, be **sensible** and make sure they add something **useful**.

- Use any **similar experiences** you've had to make your writing more **believable**.

Candidate Surname		Candidate Forename(s)	
Date		Candidate Signature	

Functional Skills

English   Level 2

Writing
Question Booklet

Time allowed: 1 hour 20 minutes

You **may not** use a dictionary.

Information for candidates
- There are **54 marks** available for this paper.
- The marks available for each question are given in brackets.

Instructions to candidates
- Use **black or blue ink** to write your answers.
- Write your name and the date in the spaces provided above.
- Read each question carefully before you start answering it.
- Answer **both questions** in the spaces provided.

Total Marks

Question 1

Remember:

For this question, you will get marks for:

- clearly and effectively communicating information

- using an appropriate amount of detail to suit the audience and purpose

- using an appropriate format and structure (including the use of paragraphs)

- using appropriate language and register for the audience and purpose

- using a range of sentence types

- using correct spelling, punctuation and grammar

- making sure your writing flows and reads well as a whole.

Question 1

It is often thought that building an airport is good for local businesses,
but bad for the surrounding environment.

- Is it likely that airports cause an increase in local trade?

- How might increased pollution and traffic congestion affect the local area?

- Should local business owners support the construction of a new airport,
  or should they leave the decision to the relevant authorities?

Writing Task

Write a report for a local business owner about the positive and negative effects
that a new airport might have on their shop and the surrounding area.

Aim to write about 250 to 300 words.

27 marks

You can use this space to plan or draft your answer:

Write your report below:

....

....

....

....

....

....

....

....

....

....

....

....

....

....

....

....

....

....

....

....

....

....

....

....

....

....

....

....

....

....

....

....

....

....

....

....

(27 marks)

Question 2

Remember:

For this question, you will get marks for:

- clearly and effectively communicating information

- using an appropriate amount of detail to suit the audience and purpose

- using an appropriate format and structure (including the use of paragraphs)

- using appropriate language and register for the audience and purpose

- using a range of sentence types

- using correct spelling, punctuation and grammar

- making sure your writing flows and reads well as a whole.

Question 2

You and a friend have just finished a two-night stay at the award-winning Buttercup Hotel.
A travel magazine has contacted you to ask if you would send them a review of your stay.
They would like to know what you liked or disliked about your stay, how the hotel could
have improved your stay and whether or not you would recommend the Buttercup Hotel.

Writing Task

Write the review described above.

Aim to write about 5 to 8 paragraphs.

27 marks

You can use this space to plan or draft your answer:

Write your review below:

....

....

....

....

....

....

....

....

....

....

....

....

....

....

....

....

....

....

....

....

....

....

....

....

....

....

....

....

....

....

....

....

....

....

....

....

....

....

....

(27 marks)

Writing Practice Paper

Answers

Part 1 — Reading

Section One — How Ideas Are Presented

Page 5

Q1 To explain about the choir.
Examples may vary. Some examples would be 'We are a local choir who rehearse at Stanhead Community Centre', 'The choir is a charitable organisation that was set up in 2008' or 'We perform at the Stanhead Festival every year'.

Q2 You could write any two of these:
- Stanhead Festival
- Town square
- County show

Q3 2008

Page 7

Q1 b — Women shouldn't work

Q2 d — Minna Williams is wrong

Q3 Truman Williams

Q4 To argue that Minna Williams is wrong.
Examples may vary. Some examples would be 'But what she said yesterday was completely unacceptable' or 'She is a disgrace and needs to educate herself before giving her opinions to the public'.

Page 9

Q1 You could write any two of these:
- To explain to the reader about the increase in cycling.
Examples may vary. For example, 'there has been a noticeable rise in the number of people out and about on their bikes'.
- To explain to people about the benefits of cycling.
Examples may vary. For example, 'it's a great way to get around'.

- To persuade the reader to go cycling.
Examples may vary. For example, 'So why not have a go yourself?'

Q2 You could write any two of these:
- To describe the Eiffel Tower.
Examples may vary. For example, 'The Eiffel Tower is an architectural beauty'.
- To advise people about visiting the Eiffel Tower.
Examples may vary. For example, 'you need to get there early'.
- To explain to the reader about the Eiffel Tower.
Examples may vary. For example, 'Tickets cost between €2.50 and €25'.

Page 11

Q1 a) Fact
b) Opinion
c) Opinion
d) Fact

Q2 Fact
Opinion
Fact
Opinion
Fact
Fact

Q3 You could write any one of these:
- 16% of bar and pub owners noticed a significant drop in business.
- The number of heart attacks has fallen by more than 40%.

Page 13

Q1 You could write any one of these:
- The writer has exaggerated how popular Mr Warhurst is.

- The writer hasn't supported what he says with any evidence.
Examples may vary. Some examples would be 'Mr Warhurst is the best MP Gawesbury has ever seen' or 'with the support of all the locals'.

Q2 You could write any two of these:
- The writer has used forceful language.
Examples may vary. For example, 'outraged', 'horrendous', 'hideous'.
- The writer has used humour.
Examples may vary. For example, 'it made my hair greasier than a plate of chips.'
- The writer has exaggerated how bad the shampoo is.
Examples may vary. For example, 'the product itself smelt horrendous'.

Page 15

Q1 You could write any two of these:
- The writer thinks video games stop people socialising face-to-face.
Examples may vary. For example, 'Gone are the days of kids hanging out with their mates after school'.
- The writer thinks video games cause social problems.
Examples may vary. For example, 'playing these mind-numbing violent games encourages anti-social behaviour'.
- The writer thinks playing video games will make it harder when young people start working. Examples may vary. For example, 'will almost certainly make it harder for these teens when they enter the workplace'.

Q2 Same opinion: They both think video games provide some social interaction.

Different opinion: Examples may vary. For example, the writer of Text A thinks video games are 'mind-numbing', whereas the writer of Text B thinks they are 'educational'.

Page 17

Q1 Advert
Q2 You could write any one of these:
- Bullet points
- Coloured text
- Picture
- Interesting font
- The name 'Shear Hairdressing'
- The 'Cuts from £10' graphic

Q3 Webpage
Q4 You could write any of these:
- Address bar
- Search box
- Links to other pages

Q5 Article
Q6 You could write any of these:
- Headline
- Columns
- Subheadings

Q7 Email
Q8 You could write any of these:
- 'To' box
- 'Subject' box
- Send or envelope button
- Box for text

Page 19

Q1 a) Headline / Title
b) You could write any one of these:
- Grabs the reader's attention.
- Tells the reader what the text is about.

Q2 a) Subheading
b) You could write any one of these:
- Breaks up the text.
- Tells the reader what the section is about.

Q3 a) Columns
b) Makes the text easier to read.
Q4 a) Bullet points
b) You could write any one of these:
- Separates the information.
- Makes the text easier to read.

Page 21

Q1 You could write any one of these:
- Makes the important information stand out.
- Makes the reader look at it first.

Q2 You could write any one of these:
- Helps the reader know what the text is about before they have read it.
- It makes the text more interesting to read.
- Grabs the reader's attention.

Q3 c — To show it's different from the rest of the text
Q4 You could write any two of these:
- Headline / Title
- Bold font
- Coloured text
- Graphic / Logo
- Bullet points

Q5 Answers may vary. For example:
- Bullet points — break up the information.
- Bold font — grabs the reader's attention.

Page 23

Q1 A new vacuum cleaner that is about to be launched.
Q2 You could write any two of these:
- Text box
- Table
- Heading
- Subheadings
- Bullet points

Q3 Answers may vary. For example:
- Text box — makes the key features stand out.
- Table — organises data, making it easier for the reader to understand.
- Heading — summarises what the article is about.
- Subheadings — tell the reader what each section is about.
- Bullet points — break up the information.

Q4 Answers may vary. For example:
- Numbered lists
- Graphics
- Footnotes

Page 25

Q1 a — Rule of three
c — Rhetorical question
Q2 Rule of three examples: 'impressive building, fascinating history and breathtaking surroundings' or 'our beautiful castle, its beautiful grounds and the beautiful landscape.' Rhetorical question examples: 'Is there a better way to spend a day than exploring Yewbarrow Castle?' or 'who doesn't like getting lost now and again?'
Q3 c — Alliteration
Q4 Answers may vary. For example: Direct address to the reader and the rule of three.

Page 27

Q1 a) Idiom
b) Metaphor
c) Simile
Q2 a — A metaphor
Q3 It helps the reader to imagine the impact the novel had on the writer.
Q4 To reveal something without meaning to.
Q5 You could write any one of these:
- 'I feel like a child about to open their birthday presents.'
- 'Waiting for a book to be released is like getting ready to set off on an adventure'.

Page 29

Q1 a) Personal
b) You could write any one of these:
- It uses words like 'we' and 'you'.
- It says what the writers think.

Q2 b — The wedding is going to be casual
Q3 a) Informal
b) You could write any one of these:
- It sounds chatty.
- It doesn't sound serious.
- It uses shortened words.
- It uses slang.

Q4 c — It matches the style of the wedding

Page 31
Q1 Advisory
Q2 You could write any of these:
- Command words
- Clear instructions
Q3 Humorous
Q4 You could write any of these:
- Exaggeration
- Informal language
Q5 Explanatory
Q6 You could write any of these:
- Definitions of specialist language
- Stating facts and not opinions

Section Two — Finding Information From Texts

Page 33
Q1 b — To tell the reader about a horse's diet
Q2 You could write any one of these:
- Grass
- Herbs
- Weeds
Q3 d — Oats
Q4 So that the horse can drink from it.
Q5 Hay

Page 35
Q1 April 28th
Q2 Table
Q3 d — McIntyre Classic Dresser
Q4 c — £750.00
Q5 You could write any one of these:
- Standford Office Desk
- McIntyre Classic Dresser

Page 37
Q1 b — Hythes Housing
Q2 On the site of the derelict playground near to St Paul's churchyard
Q3 By visiting the online forum
Q4 A new play area
Q5 You could write any two of these:
- She says that they "can reach a solution that is acceptable to everyone".

- It is an "exciting new scheme".
- "everyone will benefit, including local people".
- "feelings are running high" over it.

Page 39
Q1 a) False
   b) False
   c) True
   d) True
   e) True
Q2 d — Eat fruit and vegetables

Page 41
Q1 a) Text B
   b) 'Try not to give one-word answers to questions.'
Q2 a) Text A
   b) 'Come up with some questions to ask at the end'
Q3 Both texts suggest that you should research the company. Text A says 'Not researching the company' is a 'mistake' and Text B says 'be sure to check out their website'.
Q4 a) False
   b) True
   c) True

The Reading Test

Page 44
Q1 a — To persuade you to book a physio session
Q2 Answers may vary. For example, 'it's likely that you will pick up an injury'.
Q3 a) You could write any one of these:
   - Email
   - Phone
   b) Text box
Q4 a) 'an old hand'
   b) 'rock-bottom'

Reading Practice Paper

Section A (Page 52)
Q1 C — To persuade people to pay for additional driving lessons

Q2 A — conversational
Q3 B — Improve your driving with OPESD
Q4 Answers may vary, for example:
- where the courses take place
- when the courses take place
- how to pay for the courses
Q5 Answers may vary, for example:
Facts:
- 'Driving instructors are now recommending that motorists should take a course of post-exam driving lessons'
- 'Economical driving reduces wear and tear on vehicles'
Opinions:
- 'Making sure you can drive safely and confidently has never been more important'
- 'OPESD are currently offering some spectacular deals'
Q6 Answers may vary, for example:
Example: 'Just passing your driving test is no longer enough.'
Effect: This makes the reader feel as though they need extra lessons to be safe on the road.
Example: 'It's a priceless investment for years of safety!'
Effect: This makes the reader feel like the lessons are worth the cost.

Section B (Page 54)
Q7 B — Getting a grip
Q8 C — They are an important part of keeping people safe.
Q9 The words are:
- shattered
- groggy
Q10 Answers may vary, for example:
- 'The following advice is all you need to make sure you stay out of danger.'
- 'it seems like there's an overwhelming number of rules of the road'
Q11 Answers may vary, for example:
- It helps the reader to engage with the document.
- It makes the instructions seem more forceful to the reader.
- It makes the reader more likely to listen to the advice.

Q12 The two quotations are:
- 'rest until you feel more alert'
- 'stopping for a rest every few hours can revive your energy levels'

Q13 The features are:
- The 'Road Signs' tab / menu button
- The 'road signs' hyperlink

Q14 B — To educate
E — To instruct

Section C (Page 56)

Q15 Answers may vary, for example:
How the ideas differ:
- The documents suggest different ways for drivers to improve their road safety knowledge. Document A says that drivers can take 'post-exam driving lessons to improve their driving skills'. Document B says that drivers can find the Highway Code and take refresher tests 'online for free'.
- Document A does not give details on proper vehicle maintenance, while Document B does. Document A says that having less 'wear and tear on vehicles' reduces 'the chance of an accident occurring', but doesn't tell you what the signs of wear and tear are or how to fix them. Document B says that you should check specific parts of your car, such as checking that the 'tread depth on your tyres is deep enough'.

How the ideas are conveyed:
- Both documents use the idea of danger to strengthen their message. Document A mentions making 'drivers more aware of hazards', while Document B says the advice in the article will 'make sure you stay out of danger'. Presenting the idea of danger in the documents could shock the reader and motivate them to improve their safety on the road.

- Document A is an advert which uses colour and presents information more clearly in text boxes and bullet points. This attracts the reader and makes the lessons seem exciting. On the other hand, Document B is mostly black and white, and has information written under subheadings. This makes the information seem more serious, and suggests that safety on the roads is important, not exciting.

Part 2 — Writing

Section One — Writing Structure and Planning

Page 59

Q1 a) Audience: tourists
Purpose: to explain what there is to do in your town
b) Audience: your council
Purpose: to complain about the lack of recycling facilities
c) Audience: a charity shop manager
Purpose: to apply for voluntary work
d) Audience: your boss
Purpose: to persuade them to give you flexible working hours
e) Audience: newspaper readers
Purpose: to advise how to save money

Q2 a) Informal
b) Formal
c) Formal
d) Informal
e) Formal

Page 63

Q1 Answers may vary, for example:
Hi everyone,

I'd really like to go to a theme park and was wondering who wants to go to Talltown Towers with me?

I was thinking of going there on 22nd May. There's a train that leaves at 8 am that would get us to Uxley for 10 am (or if you'd prefer to drive, give me a call and I'll give you directions).

I've heard there are a lot of rides that you'll get wet on, so make sure you bring waterproofs.

If anyone wants to bring other friends, that's fine.

Finally, if we book tickets online, they're half-price.

I think it'll be a really fun day, and I hope you can all come.
Hope to see you soon,
Kate

Page 65

Q1 New coffee shops are opening every day in the UK. It is thought that the number of coffee shops will increase by 50% in just a few years.

Some people believe that the British interest in coffee began in 1978, when the first coffee shops opened in London. When it became clear that these shops were making a lot of money, more and more began appearing all over the country.

Last year, the coffee shop industry grew by around 8%, meaning that coffee shops are now worth £10 billion to the UK economy.

However, this growth may not continue. Research suggests that the number of coffee shops could reach a limit within the next few years.

Section Two — Choosing the Right Language and Format

Page 67
Q1 In your plan you should include:
- Give examples of ways you could help organise the party, for example put up the decorations or book the DJ.
- Any other suggestions you might have for the party. For example, a fancy-dress theme or organising transport home.

In your answer you should:
- Write 'To' and then 'harry.coates@azmail.co.uk'.
- Underneath, write 'From' and then your email address.
- Make sure you fill in the subject box with something suitable, for example 'Help with Christmas Party'.
- Start with a suitable opening, for example 'Hi Harry'.
- Write in paragraphs. You should use the bullet points in the question as a rough guide for what each paragraph should be about. You should use a new paragraph for each bullet point.
- Use an informal writing style because you know him personally.
- End with something like 'Speak to you soon' or 'Thanks' and your name.

Page 69
Q1 In your plan you should include:
- The reasons why you want to volunteer for the Mitterdon Community Centre, for example you want to get some work experience.
- Give examples of experience you have, for example you've done volunteer work in the past.
- Ideas about the sport or craft programme you'd like to run, for example coach a football team or teach mural painting.

In your answer you should:
- Write your name and address at the top right of the page.
- Write the date underneath your address.
- Write the full address of 'Mitterdon Community Centre' on the left-hand side of the page.
- Start with 'Dear Mrs Holt'. Do not use 'Dear Sir / Madam'.
- Use a formal writing style.
- Write in paragraphs. You could have one paragraph about why you want to volunteer for the programme, and another paragraph explaining why you're right for the role. You should use a new paragraph for each bullet point.
- End with 'Yours sincerely', because you know who you're writing to, and your full name.

Page 71
Q1 In your plan you should include:
- What the event was and why it was held, for example a charity dinner hosted by the Jane Bauer Foundation to raise money for the local hospital.
- What happened at the event, for example there was a speech by Mr James Johnson and a raffle.
- That the event was successful because it raised £2,500.

In your answer you should:
- Be formal because you're writing a newspaper article.
- Be informative and mention everything that happened at the event. For example, there were some great raffle prizes, such as a bottle of champagne and a holiday to Venice.

Page 73
Q1 In your plan you should include:
- Some advantages of the new car park. For example, it will mean there are fewer parking problems in Burnham.

- Some disadvantages of the theatre closing. For example, people will have to travel up to 50 miles to see a play.

In your answer you should:
- Be formal because you're writing a report.
- Write an introduction that introduces the issue.
- Include all the advantages and disadvantages of the closure of the theatre and the opening of the car park.
- Organise your information using bullet points or numbered lists, and subheadings.
- Include a conclusion which gives your opinion on the issue. You could write persuasively if you felt strongly one way or the other.

Page 75
Q1 In your plan you should include:
- Information about the office, for example it's friendly and welcoming.
- Information about the area, for example it's in a town where there is plenty to do.
- Some benefits of working for the company, for example you get health insurance.

In your answer you should:
- Be formal because you're writing a leaflet to get people to apply for a job.
- Include plenty of details about the company and the area where the company is located because a leaflet needs to be informative.
- Be persuasive because you're encouraging people to apply for a job at your company.
- Organise your information using bullet points or numbered lists, and subheadings.

- Write in paragraphs. You should use the information in the email and the bullet points in the question as a rough guide for what each paragraph should be about. You should use a new paragraph for each bullet point.

Page 77

Q1 In your plan you should include:
- The reasons why you should be chosen for the holiday, for example you work really hard in your job, but you can't afford a nice holiday.
- You could include worthwhile things you might have done, for example volunteered to work at a youth centre.

In your answer you should:
- Write your name and address at the top right of the page.
- Write the date underneath your address.
- Write the full address you're given on the left-hand side of the page.
- Start with 'Dear Sir / Madam' because you don't know the name of the person you're writing to.
- Use a formal writing style.
- Write in paragraphs. You could have one paragraph about the hard work that you do, and another paragraph explaining why you need a holiday.
- End the letter with 'Yours faithfully', because you don't know the person's name, and your name.

Page 79

Q1 In your plan you should include:
- Your own opinions about recycling, for example you always recycle all your waste.
- The reasons why you feel that way, for example because you are concerned about the environment.

In your answer:
- Make sure you write about the topic in the forum.
- Don't repeat what has been written already, but you can say if you agree or disagree with the comments made by Katie and Ali.
- Give your own opinions on recycling, for example you think that people should recycle, but you don't think they should be imprisoned if they don't.
- Write persuasively because you want to convince readers that your argument is right.
- You can write informally, because it's a forum comment. However, you should write in full sentences and be polite.

Section Three — Using Grammar

Page 81

Q1 a) arrived
   b) likes
Q2 a) Rabbits
   b) (The) supermarket
Q3 a) early
   b) (on) Tuesdays
Q4 a) (an) Italian restaurant
   b) (the) art gallery
Q5 a) an
   b) a
   c) an
   d) a
   e) an

Page 83

Q1 a) or
   b) because
   c) so
   d) but
   e) or
   f) and
   g) because
   h) so

Q2 Answers may vary, for example:
   Hi Jamie
   Thank you for the invite to dinner and the concert. I'll come for dinner, but I can't stay for the concert because I have to pick my brother up from work, if that's okay with you. I'll be around until my brother calls me. He finishes work at 10:30 pm, so I'll need to leave at about 10 pm.
   See you later
   Ben

Page 85

Q1 a) Therefore
   b) However
   c) For example
   d) Therefore
   e) For example
   f) However

Q2 Firstly, the main argument for banning mobile phones is that they can be harmful and cause all sorts of problems. For example, if they are used while driving, they can lead to road traffic accidents.
   Secondly, mobile phones are bad for your health. Some reports suggest that texting could cause arthritis.
   However, mobile phones have become an important part of everyday life, and they help people stay in touch with their friends and family. Therefore, I think we should think carefully about how much we use mobile phones, and try to avoid using them where possible.

Page 89

Q1 a) She had pasta for dinner.
   b) I saw a field of sheep on the way to work.
   c) We went to the festival.
Q2 a) I will make an apple crumble.
   b) He will come to football practice.
   c) They will be angry.

Page 91
Q1 a) <u>might</u>
b) <u>can</u>
c) <u>shall</u>
d) <u>should</u>
Q2 a) will
b) would
c) must
d) couldn't
Q3 a) must
b) should
c) could
d) might
Q4 Answers may vary, for example:
a) I <u>can</u> work overtime tonight.
b) Shilpa <u>won't</u> drive at night.
c) Gill <u>would</u> like the film.
d) You <u>mustn't</u> miss the deadline.

Page 93
Q1 a) There <u>is</u> one cat.
b) Priya <u>doesn't</u> work on Mondays.
c) We <u>were</u> on the train to London.
d) The men <u>have been</u> on holiday.
Q2 a) She <u>might have</u> broken her leg.
b) They <u>could have</u> cleaned the house.
c) I <u>should have</u> gone with him to the bank.

Section Four — Using Correct Punctuation

Page 95
Q1 a) <u>T</u>he trees in <u>S</u>cotland were about 50 ft high<u>.</u>
b) <u>O</u>n <u>M</u>onday she slipped and fell over crossing the river<u>.</u>
c) <u>H</u>iking isn't much fun with the wrong shoes<u>.</u>
d) <u>I</u> don't know where he is<u>.</u> <u>H</u>e might have gone shopping in <u>M</u>anchester<u>.</u>
e) <u>P</u>olar bears are known to be violent<u>.</u> <u>I</u> hope we don't see one<u>.</u>
f) <u>S</u>he advertised his sofa in the newspaper<u>.</u> <u>S</u>he sold it for £100<u>.</u>

Q2 a) Why are there so many horror films out at the moment<u>?</u>
b) It turned out that his own brother was the villain<u>!</u> That surprised everyone<u>.</u>
c) We went to see the football last night<u>.</u> The second half was amazing<u>!</u>
d) That's awful<u>!</u> We should do something about it<u>.</u>
e) How can you like that band<u>?</u> I don't think they're any good<u>.</u>
f) They've sold more records this year than last year<u>.</u> How have they done that<u>?</u>

Page 97
Q1 a) You need to add cinnamon<u>,</u> nutmeg and vanilla to the cake mix.
b) The cat<u>,</u> which looked like a stray<u>,</u> was very friendly.
c) James injured his shoulder<u>,</u> so he couldn't go bowling.
d) The bookshop sells biographies<u>,</u> thrillers and romances.
e) Although the cinema was full<u>,</u> it was completely silent.
f) Would you like chocolate chip<u>,</u> vanilla or strawberry ice cream?
g) They were going to go to the concert<u>,</u> but they missed the bus.
h) Alex Johns<u>,</u> who was my best man<u>,</u> never made it to the wedding.
i) Our team reached the finals<u>,</u> so we went out to celebrate.
j) I want chopped onions<u>,</u> lettuce<u>,</u> peppers and tomatoes in my sandwich.
k) Jim and Maher were going to London<u>,</u> but they changed their minds.
l) The flat-pack table<u>,</u> which had instructions with it<u>,</u> was easy to build.
m) The café<u>,</u> which sold lots of different types of tea<u>,</u> was very popular.

Page 99
Q1 a) haven<u>'</u>t
b) you<u>'</u>ll
c) I<u>'</u>d
d) couldn<u>'</u>t
e) you<u>'</u>re
f) didn<u>'</u>t
Q2 a) The office<u>'</u>s car park
b) The child<u>'</u>s sweets
c) The burglar<u>'</u>s fingerprints
d) The nurse<u>'</u>s uniform
Q3 a) <u>It's</u> not surprising that <u>it's</u> fallen over.
b) The team won <u>its</u> final match. <u>It's</u> unbelievable!
c) <u>It's</u> so nice to see your cat and <u>its</u> kittens.

Page 101
Q1 a) Have you read his new book, <u>'Glimpsing Heaven'</u>?
b) It's the first time I've ever seen <u>'The Woman in Blue'</u>.
c) <u>'The Sparkshire Herald'</u> is full of interesting articles.
Q2 a) <u>"Happy Birthday!"</u> we all shouted together<u>.</u>
b) The supporters shouted<u>,</u> <u>"Come on Hadych! You can do it!"</u>

Page 103
Q1 Answers may vary. For example:
To do before the interview:
• iron my shirt
• print my CV
• make a packed lunch
Q2 a) Answers may vary, but must include a colon before the three items, for example:
I've got three things left to buy for my holiday<u>:</u> sun cream, swimwear and a beach towel.
b) Answers may vary, but must include a colon before the three facilities, for example:
The sports centre has lots of facilities<u>:</u> a swimming pool, a climbing wall and a gymnasium.
Q3 a) Margaret has three children<u>:</u> Robin, Joseph and Emma.
b) Last year I visited three countries<u>:</u> Portugal, Croatia and Estonia.

c) Tim is holding a bake sale: he's raising money for charity.

d) The recipe only needed two more ingredients: parsnips and carrots.

e) Amy isn't coming to the party: she is going on holiday.

f) Petra always takes the stairs: she is terrified of lifts.

g) The dog barked loudly at the tree: it had seen a cat.

h) The greenhouse is full of fruit: strawberries, raspberries and tomatoes.

i) Erik is free on Tuesday afternoon: his French lessons have finished.

Section Five — Using Correct Spelling

Page 105

Q1 a) receive

b) science (word is spelt correctly)

c) achieve

d) fierce (word is spelt correctly)

e) friend

f) weird

Q2 Answers may vary, for example:
Because = Big Elephants Can Always Understand Small Elephants.

Page 107

Q1 a) cinemas

b) Fridays

c) brushes

d) journeys

e) babies

f) halves

g) reindeer (reindeer doesn't change)

h) monkeys

Q2 a) The boys ate all the peaches.

b) The puppies played in the leaves.

c) The branches were burnt to ashes.

d) The spies carried gadgets that looked like scarves.

Page 109

Q1 a) stopper (word is spelt correctly)

b) hopeful

c) lovely (word is spelt correctly)

d) replay

e) beautiful

f) mislead

Q2 a) He tried to help the jogger.

b) She was famous for her kindness.

c) I am putting this silliness behind me.

Page 111

Q1 a) He will write to you tomorrow.

b) Which hotel have you stayed at before?

c) You can wear this on many different occasions.

d) Do you know when you could come in?

e) I've had a lot of problems with my laptop as well.

f) Do you know the address of that company?

g) My experience has been horrible.

h) We hired you because you're professional.

i) A successful company doesn't receive complaints.

j) I will definitely use your business again.

k) It may be a leak, but I doubt it.

l) Is it necessary to do this immediately?

Page 113

Q1 a) I've got so much vocabulary to learn for my French exam.

b) The sales representative from the travel agency is very friendly.

c) Did you see Keeley's photographs from her summer holiday?

d) He had to prepare the food for his mother's party.

Q2 a) The train is always so busy on my morning commute.

b) The deadline for these assignments is in two weeks.

c) Aisha and Charlotte could finally get a mortgage.

d) You will be marked on how well you collaborate.

e) She's been awarded a scholarship by her university.

f) We need to consider the profitability of this project.

g) The flat comes part-furnished and is available now.

Page 117

Q1 a) Are there too many people on board?

b) I hope you're joking when you say you're going to buy a snake.

c) They're going to go to bed.

d) He was being careless with your car.

e) Can you teach me how to use our dishwasher?

Q2 a) They brought their dog into work.

b) They're going too far this time.

c) She wants to teach her son how to be polite.

d) I think you're tired of long hours.

e) I want to learn cooking from an expert.

f) Toby's been to the gym. Have you been going there too?

g) I bought it from that new shop over there.

h) Are your children being naughty?

i) There is the cake I brought into work.

Writing Practice Paper

Question 1 (Page 121)

There are 15 marks available for how you write your answer.
A top-level answer will:
- Communicate information clearly using a formal and polite style.
- Be long and detailed enough for its audience and purpose.
- Use an appropriate format and structure, including paragraphs and organisational features (where relevant).
- Use a range of sentence types consistently.

- Use a range of suitable vocabulary and techniques for the intended audience and purpose.
- Flow and read well as a whole.

There are 12 marks available for the spelling, punctuation and grammar of your answer.
A top-level answer will:
- Use grammar and punctuation correctly and with few errors.
- Use punctuation to give clarity and emphasis.
- Spell words, including irregular and specialist words, correctly and with few errors.

Your report should include:
- How an airport might affect local trade, e.g. 'There will be an increase in transport links to other towns and cities. This means there are likely to be more visitors shopping at local businesses.'
- How increased pollution and traffic congestion might affect the local area, e.g. 'The new airport could make the roads busier, so journey times could increase. The extra pollution might also harm wildlife.'
- Whether you think local people should support a new airport, e.g. 'The airport will create new jobs and opportunities in the area, so local people should support its development.'

You should set your report out correctly:
- Write a title to show what your report is about, e.g. 'The positive and negative effects of building a new airport'.
- Use subheadings to separate the different sections of your report.
- Group similar points together.
- Use bullet points or numbered lists to show information more clearly.
- Use tables to present data clearly.
- Use footnotes to add any extra information.

Your report should have a clear and logical structure:
- Write an introduction to explain what the report is about.
- Describe the positive effects of a new airport.
- Describe the negative effects a new airport.
- Write a conclusion to summarise how a new airport might affect the local business owner and surrounding area.
- Use paragraphs and full sentences.

Question 2 (Page 127)
There are 15 marks available for how you write your answer.
A top-level answer will:
- Communicate information clearly using a descriptive and informative style.
- Be long and detailed enough for its audience and purpose.
- Use an appropriate format and structure, including paragraphs and organisational features (where relevant).
- Use a range of sentence types consistently.
- Use a range of suitable vocabulary and techniques for the intended audience and purpose.
- Flow and read well as a whole.

There are 12 marks available for the spelling, punctuation and grammar of your answer.
A top-level answer will:
- Use grammar and punctuation correctly and with few errors.
- Use punctuation to give clarity and emphasis.
- Spell words, including irregular and specialist words, correctly and with few errors.

Your review should include:
- Whether you enjoyed your stay at the hotel or not, e.g. 'I thoroughly enjoyed my stay at the Buttercup Hotel.'
- What the hotel could improve on, e.g. 'There could have been a better selection of food at breakfast.'
- Whether or not you would recommend the hotel and why, e.g. 'I would recommend this hotel because the staff there really look after their guests.'

You should set your review out correctly:
- Write a title to show what the review is about, e.g. 'Pleasant stay'.
- You could end with your name to show who wrote the review. You could also include where you are from.

Your review should have a clear and logical structure:
- Start by explaining the things you liked and anything you didn't like about your stay in the hotel.
- Go on to offer any improvements that you think the hotel could make.
- End your review with your overall opinion of the hotel. You should include whether or not you would recommend the hotel and why.
- Use paragraphs and full sentences.

Glossary

A

Advertisement (advert)
A text type that persuades the reader to do something, for example buy a product.

Alliteration
When words that are close together begin with the same sound.

Apostrophe
A punctuation mark that shows that letters in a word are missing, or that something belongs to someone.

Article (text type)
A text type usually found in newspapers or magazines.

Audience
The person or people who read a text.

B

Bias
When a text isn't balanced and only gives one point of view.

Bullet points
A way of breaking up information into separate points in a list.

C

Caption
Text that tells you more about a graphic.

Conversational tone
Chatty writing normally found in informal texts.

D

Descriptive writing
Writing that tells the reader what something is like.

Direct address
Writing that uses 'you' to address the reader directly.

E

Explanatory writing
Writing that tells the reader about something.

Emotive language
Language that appeals to the reader's feelings.

F

Font
How letters look when they are typed, for example, **bold** or *italics*.

Footnote
Extra information at the bottom of a page. Shown by small, raised numbers or symbols within a text.

Formal writing
A type of writing that sounds serious and professional.

Forum
A webpage where people can discuss their opinions on a particular subject.

G

Graphic
A picture, diagram or chart.

I

Idioms
Commonly used sayings which have a different set meaning to the literal meaning of the words.

Impersonal writing
Writing that doesn't tell you anything about the writer's personality or opinions.

Informal writing
Writing that often sounds chatty and friendly.

Instructive writing
Writing that tells the reader how to do something.

Irony
When a writer says the opposite to what they mean.

142

L

Layout

How a text is presented on the page using different presentational features.

Leaflet

A text type, which is usually given away for free, that gives the reader information about something.

Letter

A text type written to a person, or a group of people, which is sent in the post.

Logo

A graphic associated with a business or product.

M

Metaphor

A way of describing something by saying it is something else.

P

Personal writing

Text that is written from a writer's point of view and uses emotional language and opinions. It sounds like it's talking to the reader.

Persuasive writing

Writing that tries to convince the reader to do or feel something.

Prefixes

Letters added to the start of a word which change the word's meaning.

Presentational features

Any part of the text which affects how the text looks, for example colour or bullet points.

Purpose

The reason a text is written, e.g. to persuade or to explain.

R

Report

A text type that gives information about something that has happened or might happen.

Rule of three

A list of three words or phrases used to create emphasis.

S

Silent letters

Letters which you can't hear when a word is said aloud. For example, the 'k' in 'knife'.

Simile

A way of describing something by comparing it to something else.

Slogans

Short, memorable phrases used in advertising.

Specialist words

Words specific to particular subjects or contexts.

Statistic

A fact that is based on research or surveys.

Style

The way a text is written. For example, a text may be advisory or humorous.

Suffixes

Letters added to the end of a word which change the word's meaning.

T

Tense

Whether a verb is talking about an action in the past or the present.

Text type

The kind of text, for example an advert or report.

Tone

The way a text sounds to the reader, for example personal or impersonal.

V

Verb

A doing or being word.

W

Webpage

A document located on the internet.

Index

E2CGSRA1